IN THE WAIT

How To Wait Right !

In The Wait

Denise M. Cassagnol

XULON PRESS

Xulon Press
2301 Lucien Way #415
Maitland, FL 32751
407.339.4217
www.xulonpress.com

© 2023 by Denise M. Cassagnol

All rights reserved solely by the author. The author guarantees all contents are original and do not infringe upon the legal rights of any other person or work. No part of this book may be reproduced in any form without the permission of the author.

Due to the changing nature of the Internet, if there are any web addresses, links, or URLs included in this manuscript, these may have been altered and may no longer be accessible. The views and opinions shared in this book belong solely to the author and do not necessarily reflect those of the publisher. The publisher therefore disclaims responsibility for the views or opinions expressed within the work.

Unless otherwise indicated, Scripture quotations taken from the King James Version (KJV) – *public domain.*

Scripture quotations taken from the Holy Bible, New International Version (NIV). Copyright © 1973, 1978, 1984, 2011 by Biblica, Inc.™. Used by permission. All rights reserved.

Paperback ISBN-13: 978-1-66287-853-4
Ebook ISBN-13: 978-1-66287-854-1

Endorsements

All of us are looking for answers and for our life experiences to have meaning. With her refreshing candor and humor, Denise unveils how *In The Wait* helps us to make sense of our plight and, for the first time, how greatly God cares about us. This is more than a good read; it is a road map to understanding the grace of God.

—Steven W. Jackson, Senior Pastor of Abundant Grace Church.

I have always admired how grounded Mrs. Cassagnol is in decisions that could impact hundreds of children in her service as an educator. Her positive influence as a parent, community member, leader in the church, educator, and soldier look effortless but is not. Waiting for what is intended for her has shaped who she is, and now she is sharing that knowledge with all of us. I recommend her book to gain awareness of how waiting is an act of faith that can change how you live.

—Autumn Carter, Instructional Specialist MS ELAR

Wow! What an amazing way to put it! *In the Wait*, many things happen. We build our character and learn to keep our faith and trust in the Lord. It is true that no one likes to wait. But we must learn how to wait without placing a time limit or ultimatum on God. He knows what is best for us. I know that people will be extremely excited to read *In the Wait*. In fact, I find myself right now in the waiting process. Thank you for authoring a book that will help people to successfully navigate this process.

—Sadie Torres, PhD

This book, *In the Wait*, is an exhilarating way of looking at our current daily lives. The book presents the golden rule for success in life. The simplicity of the arguments and the parallel comparisons are quite effective. They make us realize that God's purpose is what matters and that we should embrace that purpose as we wait on God. We must exercise patience and accept what God places in our paths to realign our lives. I highly recommend this insightful book that prepares us to stay encouraged during our waiting seasons.

—Roberto Gomez, Retired USA Army LTC
White Sands Missile Range, Senior Engineer Lead

The Word reminds us that there are benefits to waiting on God. When we wait, we are renewed, gain strength, fly above situations, run ahead of problems, and will walk into great blessings. In other words, we win and win mightily! In the space of waiting, I am excited to know that my waiting is not and has not been in vain, and if I faint not, I will receive all that God has for me. *In the Wait* is an encouraging reminder of this and of God's promises.

—Brenda Powell- Russell, PhD,
Center Operations Supervisor, USO El Paso

Acknowledgments

I give honor to God, who is the head of my life.
Thank you, God, for your abundant grace and favor.

To my mom for her love and encouragement.

To my husband for his love and support.

To my four amazing children who constantly
keep me grounded and smiling.

To my friend Sibrena for sharing and promoting this book.

Special thanks to all who helped with this momentous effort.

Contents

Introduction In The Wait xiii

Chapter One: Get Your Wait On. 1

Chapter Two: Not Willing To Wait (How Bad Do You Want It?) 7

Chapter Three: Hurry Up and Wait (Do not Prolong the Wait!) . . 39

Chapter Four: God Is In The Wait 57

Chapter Five: Empowered In The Wait 69

Chapter Six: Failing To Wait (The Downside of the Wait). 73

Chapter Seven: Confirm Your Wait (Questions That Position You for the Wait) 79

Chapter Eight: Make Your Wait Count 87

Chapter Nine: Wait In The Word 97

Chapter Ten: Let's Wait Together 101

Introduction

In The Wait

Who really enjoys waiting? We are living in the "I want it now" generation. With the advent of technology, it is quite possible to have access to knowledge at a much faster pace. When I was going to school, we used our Britannica Encyclopedias to acquire information for our research. Now within seconds, my sons, utilizing the internet and social media, have access to the same (if not more) information instantly. While I am thumbing through the encyclopedia, trying to get to the right page, Marlon and Tony have already pulled the information up on their phone or computer. No wonder I had a difficult time trying to sell those encyclopedias.

Who needs to wait to sift through all that information in the encyclopedia or dictionary when the internet has about everything categorized for you at a single swipe of the thumb or fingertips? We have been conditioned to believe that if we do not have to wait, then why should we? Instant gratification as opposed to waiting appears to be the way to go.

Believe it or not, the process of waiting is just as important for us to experience in this journey as the manifestation of the miracle or the answered prayer.

We do not live in a TV land world where all our problems are solved in thirty minutes. That is not reality because there is rarely any real waiting involved. Real waiting takes time. Real waiting is uncomfortable. I get it. The wait is sometimes long and arduous. I agree.

I know what you are thinking. I just want the thing that I am waiting for. A child does not want to hear the speech about the parental sacrifices made to get the toy. They just want the toy. They had waited long enough for that special gift to arrive.

We as adults tend to feel the same way. We do not like to wait. We want what we want when we want it. We do not want to go through the waiting process. But I found out that the wait can also be rewarding. It is through the wait you learn and grow. Through the wait, you find out what is in you and what you are made of. Do you feel that you are strong? Well, you will find out how strong you really are in the wait. If you really want to meet the authentic you and what motivates you and the intent of your heart, you will find out in the wait.

Life Point # 1

Real waiting is acknowledging that unless the Lord is included in the plan, then your plan is futile (Psalm 127:1-2).

Real waiting requires surrendering your control and accepting God's influence.

The wait is far from glamorous. It is not for the quick fixers or the ones looking for an effortless way out. Waiting is not an overnight sensation. Waiting takes time. Maturation and transformation happen during the wait. Things are transitioning and shifting during the wait so that the wait can provide clarity of purpose, while establishing direction and setting up wholeness and restoration. The wait helps to redefine you and your situation as it confirms your personal status of readiness for the answered prayer.

In the wait, you can connect with God as you move closer to the desired outcome. In the wait, you learn your purpose and discover the path that God has for you. God is strategic and methodical. He does not want you confused, wasting time, and wandering around in the wilderness. Instead, God wants to relay instructions for you to accomplish.

Not only does God want you to fulfill your purpose, but God wants to place you in position to develop and prepare others. Ironically, the wait is designed to teach you how to wait so that you can hear and receive from God. It is through the wait that you gain direction, reassurance, empowerment, and toughness. During the wait, God is pouring purpose into you and constructing the platform that you will use. He is also identifying a replacement that you will have the opportunity to mold.

In the wait, you get to exercise your faith muscles. Ouch, Ouch, Ouch. The stretching hurts, and it is not easy. But it is necessary to establish the mindset and discipline needed to move on to the next level or maintain while you are waiting for the manifestation of the requested prayer. Why should God bless you with a request or position of responsibility that you are not ready to receive? Why should God bless you with something that you are just going to mess up?

My daughters and I were having an intense conversation about the characteristics of a potential husband. They were saying that they wanted "a tall, financially independent, strong, dedicated, God-fearing man that loves the Lord and is focused on God's plans for his life." They acknowledged that if this man first loved the Lord, then he would allow the Holy Spirit to show him how to love them. However, if you ask God for his best for you, then you must be willing to wait on God and accept the changes that God is going to make in you as you wait. God does not want you to make a shipwreck of your life. He does not want you and others to suffer irretrievable loss and destruction. Instead, God wants you to be unwavering and prevail as He helps you traverse through the storms.

The wait shows you if you are ready for the thing that you are requesting and if you are ready for the work that God has assigned for you. If you are not, then the wait will reveal this, too, and what you need to do to get ready for the blessing.

The military and other organizations conduct inspections to determine the unit's state of readiness. The idea behind the inspection is to reveal to that unit where they stand and what needs to be done to correct the deficiencies. The inspection helps the unit to establish specific safeguards within certain time limits. If the unit needs to tighten up their security procedures or administrative or operational functions, then the deficiencies or shortcomings will be discovered during the inspection.

The inspection's main goal should always be to bring that unit to readiness. The purpose should never be to hurt or catch the organization off guard. Although "*got-you-isms*" and blame do occur, they really do not help to solve the immediate concern. They only serve to muddy up the water and detract from mission readiness. Accountability, not retaliatory measures, are necessary to ensure that problems are resolved. Once you are aware of the faults, you can adjust and work to fix the roadblocks. If more training is needed, then implementation of that training must be scheduled and conducted.

Like an inspection, the wait shows you the weaknesses and shortcomings that serve as obstacles. During the wait, God is not trying to beat you up or put you on blast. Instead, God wants to show you where you are and what you need to do to get to the point that you can contend with the answered prayer. God had the answer to your prayer the moment that you prayed it. He already knew what your need was. Get this! Not only does God have the answer to your prayers, but He is ready to deliver on the promise.

So, what is the holdup? Well, I can guarantee that the holdup is not God. God is ready and willing to move you to the next level. God does not want you inactive or complacent. He wants you to be active and work for Him. Unfortunately, we are the holdup. We are not waiting for God as much as He is waiting for us. God is always ready—are you?

If God serves the expected gift or requested prayer before you are ready to receive it, then you will not be as successful or blessed as you could have been if you were prepared and ready. As a result of not being ready, you might regress instead of moving forward. The fact that you are not ready may not only affect you. Others may be impacted as well. So, we need to be ready and seasoned to receive the thing that God has in store for us. We must be ready and prepared for the things that we are asking God to do in our lives. We just cannot keep saying "Gimme, gimme, gimme" and not be ready. Do not have your hand out and not be prepared.

When do you get ready? How do you prepare? The answer is in the wait.

Chapter 1

Get Your Wait On

Lamentations 3:24 says that *"The Lord is my portion."* Stop!

If I had a dollar for every time, I failed to acknowledge God or wait for him to fix situations in my life, I would be a zillionaire by now. Believe me, that adage is applicable. Yes, I own my willful stubbornness. And what really turns an unpleasant situation into a tragic one is that in each instance, I knew better.

I heard songs sung, messages preached, mommy words spoken, and genuine concern shared from real friends. I have read the Bible, and I have seen the ramification of sin working in the lives of the presumptuous. But I still made the decision to echo my life after the late *Frank Sinatra* and say, *"I Did It My Way!"* Sad, but true.

Now, I am not saying that every time I decided to be proactive, my actions led to horrendous results. But it follows that if I had first yielded to the Holy Spirit, I would have discarded my arrogance and received greater clarity and vindication.

When the Lord is my portion, He becomes my destiny. The Lord is automatically in control of my life. The Lord is my fate. More specifically, the Lord is my strength; He is my provider and shepherd. The Lord is my cover and my defense! He is my peace and my ticket to wholeness! The Lord is my joy and my hope! Everything that I have and everything that I am is all because of Him. God receives the credit. The thought of my very existence clings to God's purposes for my life.

The bottom line is: The Lord is my everything! God is my end game! Why is God all these things? The song by Michael W. Smith sums up who God is perfectly by saying that God is a "*Way Maker, Miracle Worker, Promise Keeper, Light in the Darkness.*" He brilliantly uses these titles to describe God in the song "*Way Maker*"! There is no getting around the fact that without God, you have nothing! Without God, you are on a bullet train, going nowhere fast! Without God, metaphorically speaking, you are just another player in the Squid Game of Life.

Having established that brutal fact, I have no other choice but to wait on Him. In other words, I choose to actively pursue God's path and choices for me. Now, that is a lot easier said than done. There have been times in my own life when I wanted to quit because I did not see how my situation was going to change for the better.

Wrestling with problems in the lives of my children, personal finances, physical and verbal abuse, negative thinking, lustful heart, unfulfilled dreams, church hurt, fear and insecurity, and betrayal kept my baggage packed and ready. All those things beat down my passion and colored my perception. Instead of looking at obstacles through God's lenses, I am squinting and trying to see in the dark. Focusing on the negativity of poor choices leads to misdirection and calamity.

On many occasions, I stopped praying and started doubting God. Since God had not answered when I wanted Him to or in the way that was comfortable for me, I felt it was appropriate to take matters into my hands. But in my inevitable yet chaotic metamorphosis (in other words, repeated self-driven train wrecks), I tearfully stumbled back to my only place of consolation. Therefore, I learned through my pain that the Lord rewards those who selflessly wait on Him. I learned that the Lord miraculously cleans up the stain of my pain and transforms my liabilities into abilities that I can use for Him. God shaped my pain into an employable platform that can be used for Him.

That is what the second part of that scripture says. "The Lord is my portion: *therefore, I will wait for Him.*" In other words, I will depend on God. I will rely on God. I will seek after His ways. I will move according to God's plan and schedule.

Waiting on the Lord is like waiting for a certain bus to take you to your desired destination. As you ride the bus, you know that there will be twists and turns. There will be stops and starts, but eventually you expect to arrive at your journey's end. Knowing that the Lord holds my destiny (portion), I will wait on God because He provides and equips the one who waits with what is needed to successfully arrive at God's chosen destination. No matter how many bumps or pits or cracks and holes along the journey, God employs the necessary adjustments to prevent you from missing the goals or path that He has for you. God is in control, and you can trust Him with your future.

Surely, I am not trying to tell you how to live your life or that your life will suddenly become perfect as you are waiting for God. I can only say that when I reflect on my testimony, personal manipulation, and opposition to God's way of doing things never worked for me. Through countless episodes (I could host my own reality TV show or be the subject of a sitcom), I learned that the safest place to be is where God is. When I did not wait, I got off track and experienced missed opportunities.

Life Point # 2

Waiting on the Lord means that you recognize that he who began a good work in you will be faithful to perform it until the day of Jesus Christ (Philippians 1:6).

Moses told God that he would not move unless God moved with him. Moses said in **Exodus 33:15, "that if your presence does not go with us then do not send us up from this place."** God had to reassure Moses that he would be with him. **In verse 16, God said, "That my presence will go with you, and I will give you rest."**

When we wait for God, God directs us. When God directs us and we follow that direction, we will have rest. When we wait for God, we are in action mode. Too many times, we think that the word *wait* means to become inactive or passive. That word, wait, means to stay where you are until something happens. An acronym for the word wait is **W**hen **A**nswer **I**s **T**ransparent. If the way is not clear, don't move. Wait! Remember, while you are waiting, you are still actively living.

David understood the importance of remaining in the role of a shepherd, Jonathan's friend, husband, brother, and a warrior until God chose the right time to elevate him as the king of Israel.

Now when you are waiting on God, you are planted, not stagnated. There is a notable difference! The word *stagnated* means that there is no movement. There is no activity. Like water that is stationary, there is no current and the water does not flow. As a result, the water stinks, festers, creates mold, and breeds mosquitoes. Like a dead body with no blood flowing in the veins, the body smells, rots, and decomposes.

However, when a person is planted and waiting in the Lord, that person is constantly growing in the ways of the Lord. There may be some delays, but eventually the waiting process will yield a Christ-like product. When you are planted in the Lord, you learn to trust God and exemplify the fruit of the spirit.

Life Point # 3

Like David, we need to ask the Lord for guidance and direction. Ask God to show you the right path to follow and then wait on him (Psalm25:4-5).

But The fruit of the Spirit is love, joy, peace, longsuffering, gentleness, goodness, faith, meekness, temperance: against such there is no law. (Gal. 5:22–23) (NKJV).

Pastor Andrea Moore of Summit Church in Austin, Texas, and author of *God Took a Day Off: Why Can't I?* said at her She Waits

Women's Conference, "We need to wait *in* God as opposed to waiting *on* God. When we wait *in* Him, we are incapsulated (sheltered) in Him."

Think of a mother carrying her baby in her body. While the baby is in the womb waiting, it is protected and sheltered from harm. The baby is nourished, developed, and is being prepared for life outside the womb. When we are waiting and trusting in God, we are being nourished, strengthened, developed, and prepared for life paths. God knows the proper timing to bring His plans to fruition in us.

As you are planted, you are being watered and nurtured with the right soil for harvest and seed reproduction. Like a flower or crop fertilizing in the soil, you do not necessarily see the daily growth process. But you trust that you have planted that seed *in* the right soil so that it will grow and continue the birth process. Nevertheless, as the flower or crop is resting in the soil's watered nutrition, it soon blooms. That planted crop eventually produces an expected harvest.

When you wait for God, you will eventually bloom, come to fruition, and produce a fruitful harvest. When you wait for God, you will not spiritually rot or decompose. Instead, when you wait for God, you will give birth, yield an anticipated harvest, and be complete in Him. In the wait, God teaches you how to wait on Him, recognize His voice, and use discernment. In the wait, God shows you how to yield and be directed by His Holy Spirit.

I want God to be creative with me and design for me as I yield to Him, an unexpected yet an abundant harvest. I want a fulfilled and Christ-enhanced life. Like Jabez, I want God to "enlarge my territory."

> Lord, forgive me for the times that I moved ahead of You or for the times that I refused to do things according to Your ways. Forgive me for not acknowledging You for the many doors that You opened and not having the courage to go through. Help me to get my wait on so that I will be ready to receive the blessing and be a blessing to others. I desire to be complete in You.

In The Wait

When was the last time you waited for a change or for something that you wanted? How long did you wait? Were you able to maintain composure or did you rant and rave? Waiting right is much easier when you trust God and allow Him the time needed to fix things for you. God can do great and wonderful things. He has been known to change the unchangeable and reverse the irreversible.

We should choose to wait on God. We should not want God to do miraculous things for us or tell Him to have His way when we really do not want to wait for God to equip us and fix our situation. Why pretend to wait on God if you are just going to do things your way anyway. Instead, we need to ask God to help us to wait the right way. If we wait right, then we will gain more than just a tangible product. God wants to give you more than what you are asking or thinking. God yearns to perform miracles and turn things around for you. We must trust and wait on Him.

So, get your wait on!

Life Point # 4

Think of the Holy Spirit as our personal life coach, chief mentor or trainer supporting, guiding, and helping you to thrive as you go through life.

Chapter 2

Not Willing to Wait

(How Bad Do You Want It?)

Ask people if they think that it would be better to wait on God or do their own thing. Most would say, without reservations, it is better to wait on God. Some of those same people might even start preaching or sharing their tearful testimony and life experiences about the times when they followed their destructive choices. They would finally admit that they should have allowed God to have His way in their lives. In hindsight, they would boldly say "G-I-R-l, wait for the Lord and let Him take care of things for you!" The Bible admonishes every reader to do the same.

"Wait on the Lord: be of good courage, and he shall strengthen thine heart: wait, I say, on the Lord" *(Ps. 27:14).*

So, if we are to wait on God, then why don't we? If the thing that we are asking God for is important, then why not wait on God to provide? Why resort to half-baked schemes and manipulation? Many times, you do not get what you want. And if you do get a reasonable facsimile, it always would have been better if you would have received it God's way. How bad do you want what you are asking or believing God for? You would think that if what you are waiting for is significant and worth pursuing, then you should automatically be willing to wait on the Lord for the manifestation.

I have asked people why they chose to move forward with their plans as opposed to waiting on God. The answers are varied, ranging from simple to complex. After evaluating their reasons for not waiting on God, a common pattern unfolds. The common thread or mistake in achieving what we desire is the idea that we have the personal power via skills, knowledge, talents, achievements, and experience to create the things we want. We feel that we do not have to wait on God to do things for us because we have what it takes to do things for ourselves. Due to our personal nature and abilities, we often do not feel that it is necessary to wait on God. Unfortunately, this misconception has forecasted dire consequences and a losing dynamic for us. The crux of the matter is that we need to consult God and wait on Him.

However, the reasons people said that they do not wait are:

Reason 1 God Takes Too Long!

We quote the phrase, "God may not come when you want Him, but He's always on time!" But do you really believe it? Be honest! You are in a safe place. Or maybe when we are in the reflective process of justifying our actions, we selectively hear only the first part which is, "God may not come," Period.

Consequently, instead of having the courage to wait, we jump wholeheartedly into the mix. We gave God some time (really), and since God has not shown up (blame God), we have no other choice (denier) but to choose options (limited and narrow focus) that we think (pride) are best (bias) for us. In other words, we put God on our timetable rather than waiting for the activation of His schedule or plan. We simply become despondent after God has not responded to our request according to our timetable.

Unfortunately, our timetable is based on a few days or weeks. We get flustered when God takes his time. Like addicts, we start getting shaky and look for ways to help ourselves solve the problem. We throw up the request, and then we take out our watches. Get ready, get set, go! Tick-tock, tick-tock.

As we play the *Jeopardy* theme song in our mind, we wait compulsively for God to answer our prayer. We want God to perform a miracle. We spend time playing the wrong scenarios in our minds as we try to figure out the reason for God's delay. We even try to negotiate appropriate outcomes. "God if you give me this, then this will happen. If you change this, then I will be able to do that."

We often predict the worst as we position ourselves to act spontaneously. "If God has not moved by this time, then I will fix it myself!" Time passes and nothing has changed. We ask, "When is God going to answer my prayer? When is God going to fix things for me?"

We tragically convince ourselves that life is going to pass us by if we do not quickly move to self-resolution. Make the choice! Do something! Tick-tock, tick-tock. The date that you marked on the calendar has passed, and you have received constant reminders from significant others that time is fleeting. "What are you doing to make things happen?" "How much longer are you going to wait on God to make things happen for you?" "God helps those who helps themselves! "You'd better get out there and go after that dream before it's too late!"

Here's where the rush cycle begins. Reflect on a request or prayer you have waited on God to provide and fill this out (fill in the blanks):

You'd better _____ before _____ gets it or before _____ happens.

Can you hear your friend's voice yelling ultimatums as you wait for the manifestation of the promise? How about the voice of a boss, sibling, parent, or spouse influencing you to be responsible and to take charge of your situation? What is your inner voice telling or pushing you to do?

I remember crying my heart out, waiting for the Lord to move on my request for a company command. Officers were told that it would take at least one year of working within the command structure before you would be considered for a company command. During that time, you should become familiar with the unit's mission and become a seasoned captain. Well, almost eighteen months had passed, and I still did not have a command. One of my colleagues admonished me to act. When I told her I was praying and waiting on God, she said, "Praying! You had better get out there and let those battalion commanders know that you are interested in taking command." Suddenly, praying and waiting on God seemed secondary. I needed to "up" my game. I needed to move out now regardless of God's plan for me. Even though, I interviewed for different commands and prayed, waiting for God to work things out for me quickly dissolved. I had to have a command when I wanted it.

I continued to schedule interviews for the position but to no avail. My husband tried to console me, but with each rejection notice or call, my heart sank. I kept hearing about the success of others while wondering when I was going to get my turn. It seemed like all my friends were getting commands. Although I was happy for them and I attended their change of command ceremonies, I still wanted my turn. My husband told me to keep on working and trusting God. Eventually, I stopped crying. I stopped complaining. It was time to step out on faith and believe God for my request, no matter how long it took.

I had been in Germany for over two years, and I still had not received a command. Another colleague told me that God was going to grant my request, but it would not be at my assigned brigade. Nevertheless, I was still trusting God. I had already been interviewed outside the brigade. I remember telling God to have His way. I had done all I could do. The ball was in His court, and I would accept His plan for my life. Finally, it happened. I accepted a command offer. This offer came from outside my brigade about eight months prior to my permanent change of station.

That is right, about eight months before I was scheduled to go to a brand-new assignment, God answered my prayer. It took over two years, but God gave me a command. God gave me the right people within the command to work with and the right bosses to work for. God had lined everything up perfectly. My area of command responsibility was far greater in this new assignment than it would have been if I had received a command in my last unit. The number of people in my command had more than tripled in size from those of my friends and peers who already had their commands. Even my appraisal exceeded expectations from both my rater and senior rater. Look at God!

"He is the one you praise; he is your God, who performed for you those great and awesome wonders you saw with your own eyes" (*Deut. 10:21*) **(NIV).**

Everyone gets to fill in the blanks according to their personal circumstances. The blanks are endless. The voices in your head along with the people in your life are relentlessly screaming that the time to move is now. Your inner salesperson tells you that if you do not act right now, then you are going to miss out! When you look at your situation, you begin wondering why you are still waiting. You begin telling yourself that everybody else has already made their moves. If you have found yourself on that spinning top, waiting days and days and days, questioning when or if God is going to answer your prayer or request, let me help you.

"This is the confidence we have in Him, that if we ask anything according to his will, he hears us. And if we know that he hears us whatever we ask- we know that we have what we asked of him" (*1 John 5:14–15*).**(NJKV)**

God does not need a hearing aid. He heard you the first time you prayed. You can, but you do not have to constantly remind Him. God does not have dementia. Unlike us, He is not forgetful. In fact, He already knew what you were going to ask before you asked. He remembers everything. God is going to respond according to His timing.

"But do not forget this one thing, dear friends: With the Lord a day is like a thousand years, and a thousand years are like a day" (*2 Pet. 3:8*) (NIV).

Wow, that means God's rate of response is not on the same pace as ours. We are crying about God taking too long or moving too slow when the reality is that God is not too slow. He is moving to His pace and not ours. This scripture refers to God's promise of the return of our Lord and Savior. God does not want people to think because He has not yet returned, that God is slow or slack in performing His Word. Quite the contrary. God is just being patient to allow for more people to accept Him.

I would like to think that the same premise is in operation when it comes to God working things out for us. God in His timing, not ours, plans to address our concerns and meet our needs. The wait is certainly not because God needs the time to get ready. The wait is not because God needs His heart and attitude adjusted. The wait is not because God needs to be equipped or finetuned for the mission. But, rather, the "wait" is often due to *our* not really being fully ready or in the right position to receive the request, commitment, or blessing.

Sometimes we may think that we understand what God is thinking or doing when we do not. We do not think or put things together like God.

"For my thoughts are not your thoughts, Nor are your way My ways," declares the Lord" (*Isa. 55:8-9*).

Sometimes, the wait has nothing to do with us. The wait has something to do with God using our trials to encourage someone else. God could also be using the wait time to set the stage for our success. Understand that God stands ready, willing, and able to do **"exceedingly and abundantly above all that we ask or think according to the power that works in us) (Eph. 3:20).**

As God works in us and others, He is preparing the "right situation" at the "right timeframe" to manifest His plan and purpose in our lives. So, the next time we become despondent, disappointed, or disillusioned because God has not met our expiration date, then remember God is always working things out for our good. God is not sleeping or on vacation. God wants us to succeed. God wants us to have the victory in our lives.

Yes, God could easily snap His fingers, blink, speak and immediately transform our request into reality. However, if you are not ready to receive the promise, then you will be set up for failure. God does not glory in your failure. God is a good, just, and righteous God. His faithfulness is everlasting, and His mercy endures through all generations.

What loving parent would place their child behind the wheel of a car and tell them to drive before they are ready. Yes, that child wants to have the car. Yes, that child thinks they are ready to drive. If the child drives before they are ready, they can cause destruction, mayhem, and death. If we do not wait on God, we can cause destruction, mayhem, and death. The best way to be ready, successful, and achieve the desired goal is not to rush or go before we are ready. Instead, we must wait on God's timing.

When Moses went up to the mountain to hear from God and to receive instructions, he had to wait. After waiting six days, God told Moses to proceed up the mountain. God was ready to speak to Moses. On the seventh day, Moses entered the cloud and climbed to the top of Mt. Sinai. He stayed with God for forty days. During this time, Moses received the Lord's commandments on two stone tablets.

"When Moses went up to the mountain the cloud covered it, and the glory of the Lord settled on Mount Sinai. For six days the cloud covered the mountain and on the seventh day the Lord called to Moses from the cloud" (*Exod. 24:15-16*)(NIV).

We must realize that waiting on God often takes time. However, the rewards and the advantages of waiting on God far outweigh the disadvantages and problems that occur when choosing not to wait on God.

Reason 2 God Is Too Busy to worry about My Problem(s)

God is busy and has the responsibility of the world on His shoulders. He works nonstop. Just keeping me straight is a full-time job. There are approximately eight billion people on the earth. Everybody has difficulties. Now imagine God overseeing those problems plus the obstacles affecting the world.

"The earth is the Lord's, and the fullness thereof; the world, and they that dwell therein" (*Ps. 24:1*).

God has a lot on His plate, but He is never too busy or overwhelmed to see about issues affecting you. The earth belongs to God, and so do you. God can oversee all of earth's problems, including your predicaments.

When I think about biblical characters who had tough challenges, I think about Moses. I see Moses holding his heavy arms up with the help of Aaron and Hur until sunset (Exod. 17:12). When Moses's arms were raised, the Israelites experienced victory. When Moses's arms dropped, the Israelites suffered defeat. So, all three were aware of the great responsibility they had in keeping Moses's arms lifted during the battle. They were busy throughout the battle, holding Moses's arms up and more than likely keeping him encouraged. Unlike Moses, God does not need any assistance. Your concerns are not too large or small for Him. God is never too busy to come to your aid.

Can you imagine the tremendous responsibility of God? Let me tell you that we cannot! We cannot begin to fathom the huge responsibility. We are not even aware of all that God has on His plate. But just know this, that God can control everything while taking care of everybody. He is omniscient, omnipresent, and omnipotent. God knows when and where something is going to happen. He is already there when it is happening, and He can either prevent it or bring it to fruition. God is so powerful that He can simply speak things into existence. If God thinks it, it is done!

Even though God has a lot to look after, He is still mindful of you and your needs. The song by Civilla Martin says, "His eye is on the sparrow." If God sees the smallest of birds, then you know that He sees you. God watches over us to provide, protect, and perform His will in us. God has never been too busy to assist you with your concerns. God loves hearing from you and wants to answer your prayers. God is always available and longs to commune with you.

Life Point # 5

Omniscient = all – knowing
omnipresent = all – present (everywhere)
Omnipotent = all – powerful

The enemy wants us to believe that God is too busy so that we will not take the necessary time to communicate with God. But if you say it, God hears it. Even before you speak it, God has summed up your story. God is the author and finisher of our faith (Heb. 12:2). He wisely interprets the intents of the heart and is a discerner of our every thought (Heb. 4:12).

Did you know that God wants to have a relationship with you? He is just waiting for you to reach out and connect with him. So, the question is not if God is too busy. Instead, the question is, are we too busy to talk to God about our problems? Here it comes. Are you entangled by the vicissitudes of life?

You have three jobs, six dogs, five kids, and are still working in various church ministries. Talking about having a great deal to do. I know that that is an exaggeration. But we really do need to stop associating our busyness with God. Because you are too busy, you automatically think that God is too busy. That is transference. Because we are so caught up in minutiae, we think God is also overcome by events.

Life Point # 6

The Lord is waiting on us to come to Him. Stop driving the car over the cliff! Get off that vicious roller coaster! God wants to converse with you As He shares His point of view on life. God wants to set you up for success.

Because you are the one who is so busy, when do you have the time or take the time to talk to God about anything? When was the last time you asked God for His opinion or plan before you arbitrarily rolled out what you wanted to do.

Yes, God is busy handling universal issues, but He is not too busy for you. He is not like man. Man may have difficulty multitasking at times, but not God. Man may have difficulty dealing with insurmountable odds, but God is not deterred by the size of any impediment. God is not intimidated and does not play games. There is no mountain that can stop Him. He will just move the mountain. He is God and He can take care of everything on His own.

Joyce Meyer says, "*That God wants to do life with Us.*" Wow, that is profound! As much as I mess up stuff, God wants to be with me. God is not too busy to come to see about me. In my imperfection, God wants to be with me. In my messed up past, God still has a platform and a purpose for me. Thank you, Lord! Not only does God want to take the time to have a quality relationship with us on this side of heaven, but He wants to have an eternal relationship with us as His children (1 Tim. 2:3). What an honor! We need to be glad about that!

Martha Munizzi sings a song called "Your *Latter Shall Be Greater Than Your Past.*" God wants to tell you that your latter days, the days that will come later, the days that have not come yet, will be greater than your past. She sings that "You will be blessed more than you can ask. Despite all that has been done, your best is yet to come. Your future will be better than your past."

"The glory of the latter house shall be greater than of the former, saith the Lord of Hosts: and in this place will I give peace, saith the Lord of hosts" (*Hag. 2:9*).

God wants to tell you to hang in there. God is still sovereign, and He is still sitting on the throne. He is never too busy for you. He is reaching out to you and wants to hear from you today. He is reaching out to you and wants to offer you His peace and resolution.

"What is man that God is mindful of him, And the son of man that you visit him?" (*Ps. 8:4*).

Think about that. God thinks about us. God, in all the things that He must do, has us on His mind. As busy as God may be, God is willing to take the time out to spend with us. When He spends time with us, He wants to hear about the things that are important to us. He wants to hear about your hurts and your accomplishments, your discouragement and what assures you, your tears, and dreams. He wants to hear about your likes and dislikes. I think that God will even listen to your jokes. God will take the time to not only listen to what is important to you, but He also wants to share His divine plans.

"For I know the plans I have for you," declares the Lord, "plans to prosper you and not harm you, plans to give you hope and a future" (*Jer. 29:11*).

Reason 3 God Does not Care about Me

This is one of the biggest reasons that people give for not waiting on God. Is it self-pity, guilt, arrogance, ignorance, or shame that makes you feel that God no longer loves or cares about you? Do not let the enemy brainwash you into thinking that God does not care. Get a grip!

"Therefore the Lord waits to be gracious to you, and therefore he exalts himself to show mercy to you. For the Lord is a God of justice; blessed are all those who wait for him" (*Isa. 30:18*).

The Lord wants to be gracious to you. The word *gracious* means kind, merciful, and forgiving. Who among us does not need kindness, mercy, or forgiveness? I know I do. Thank God for His impeccable goodness and His abundant grace. Because God cares about our fears and is concerned about us, He purposely looks for ways to bless us and make our lives better and more meaningful. We should be ecstatic and grateful that God cares enough about us to order our steps and continually provide for us. God is always looking out for us. Our success is based on what God wants to place in motion for us. God cares so much about us that He desires to take care of our concerns, hurts and problems. He wants to help us overcome the hurdles we experience.

Give all your worries and cares to God, for he cares about you" (*1 Pet. 5:7*).

God is not a fair-weather God. Like fans at a sporting event, most fans will show up and cheer for their teams if it is not too cold or raining. Thankfully, God is not like that. God will show up no matter what. You need God to provide for you and your family. No problem. God anxiously yearns to do just that. He makes provisions for the things that you need.

"But my God shall provide all your needs according to his riches and glory by Christ Jesus" (*Phil. 4:19*).

Why? Because he cares. A person who does not care about you will not be bothered to give you anything. Sometimes people who do care are unable to give you what you need. God is not in that category. God cares about what happens to you. That is why we need to be transparent and include Him. Tell Him and then trust Him for the things that you need.

(Give your burdens to the Lord, and he will take care of you. He will not permit the righteous to be moved (*Ps. 55:22*) **(NJKV).**

Unfortunately, there are people that will push you to make you fall. They will set traps and devise schemes to make you lose focus and distract you. Believe me, a person who does not care about you will not be bothered to treat you fairly. They will use every avenue to get rid of you and make you look bad. They will use you and run roughshod over you. They will be aggressive and abrasive toward you. They do not care about your feelings or the things that matter to you. But God will take care of you and not let their evil plans become an albatross around your neck.

"The Lord directs the steps of the Godly. He delights in every detail of their lives. Though they stumble, they will never fail, for the Lord holds them by the hand." (*Ps. 37:23-24*) **(New Living Translation-NLT).**

Think about that. Who do you honestly know that delights or takes joy in every aspect of your life? Who do you know that really wants to hear about every aspect? Now if you are dishing dirt or exposing secrets, then everyone has time for that. Talk to your parents, friends, or spouse about your fishing trips, new job, your kid's first steps, weight loss, finances, projects, sermons, or sickness and see how long people stay with you. Some people will not pick up the phone when their favorite shows are on. You better not have a problem when *The Bold and the Beautiful* or *Judge Judy* comes on! God does not have a favorite program that prevents Him from caring about you.

My mom does not like to talk for a long time on the phone. That's why when I call her, I try to push everything that has happened with me, Tony, kids, grandkids, job, and the ministry in about twenty minutes or less. I can talk fast. I know that after twenty minutes, she's ready for you to wind down so she can get off the phone. My mom loves me, but eventually, she will start thanking me for calling so she can quickly take her exit. Thank God, we can take our time to talk with God. God does not get bored. He never reminds us that "You already said that!" God is so understanding. You do not have to hang up the phone on Him because He has been insensitive and hurt your feelings. God does not have selective hearing. When you call, God picks up. It does not matter what time you contact Him. He is always available.

"Call to me and I will answer you and tell you great and unsearchable things you do not know" (*Jer. 33:3*) (*NIV*).

Life Point # 7

Sometimes, like the prophet Elijah, we are spiritually, mentally, physically, and emotionally exhausted (1ˢᵗ Kings 19: 1-4).

If that is you, then ask God to show you how to achieve balance. God cares and will provide guidance, restoration, refreshing and wholeness.

God cares about your shortcomings, faults, and everything that you are going through. God is not just there when everyone is celebrating you. He is there during the chaos and demanding times too.

"When you go through deep waters, I will be with you. When you go through rivers of difficulty, you will not drown. When you walk through the fire of oppression, you will not be burned up; the flames will not consume you" (*Isa. 43:2*).

During adversity, God is with you. He will never leave you or forsake you. Even at times when we do not have it all together, God is still working things out for us. Remember God cares for you and cherishes the time that you spend together. God said draw nigh, or near, to me and I will draw nigh or near to you (James 4:8). God will not leave you hanging. He will provide for you. God has you and all that He has created in His capable and loving hands. When you feel burned out, unsure, and weak, God is your best source for respite, wisdom, and strength.

God has always cared for you and will provide for the things that you need. A trick of the enemy is to make you think that God does not care. Satan is the one who does not care and wants to see you nullified and destroyed. Do not let others falsely persuade you that they can do a better job of looking after you than God. You are just setting yourself up for disappointment and disillusionment. Even with their best intentions, no one can do you like the Lord. Do not let others make you feel that they care for you more than God. There are certain habits or idiosyncrasies that you have that are annoying to say the least. Besides your mother, very few can tolerate you for extended periods. You have lost relationships because of habits and different points of view. Friends and family may have left you, but God is still with you. God loves you, and He cares about you more than you can imagine. We know that God cares about the big things, but God also cares about the smallest of your concerns.

Therefore, take no thought, saying, what shall we eat? Or What shall we drink? Or Wherewithal shall we be clothed? (For after all these things do the Gentiles seek for your heavenly Father knoweth that ye have need of all these things)" (*Matt. 6:31-32*).

Reason 4 God Is Tired of My Mistakes

And your point is? Yes, you have made mistakes, but that does not mean that God has given up on you. In fact, God is the only one who has not admitted defeat. When the boxer's coach throws the towel into the ring during the boxing match, the fight is over. Go home, lock up, and turn off the lights. But God has not surrendered. God has not turned His back on you. He is not through with you. God still desires to salvage the situation and cause you to do greater things for Him.

God knows how to take your mistake and turn it around so that He still gets the glory. He knows how to make platforms out of all our foiled plans. Understand that one "yes" from God makes the devil's "no" null and void. If someone has announced your ruin because of your mistake, God will say "Hold up" and "Not Yet." God can cancel any of the devil's plans. Although others may abandon you, God is not going to run out on you because of your flaws. God knows your weaknesses, and He is prepared to meet you where you are and fix those shortcomings. God knows how to configure the stage despite judgment and condemnation. God operates under an at-will policy. According to God's will, it is going to happen.

If you have fallen, God will continue to give you an opportunity to get back up. The key is to learn something from the mistake. Hopefully, you learned not to repeat the same mistakes but also how to do things better. If I get hurt because I am jumping down the steps, guess what, I am going to stop jumping down the steps. First, it hurts. Second, I am going to learn from that experience. Now, if that or a comparable situation occurs again, I am going to be prepared. I am not going to blindly go through that again. Because I have learned from my previous experience, I am going to talk to God to make sure that He is going to be with me. This time, I will be better prepared to deal with the obstacles. I will have the right focus, training, equipment, and available support systems prior to taking the risk. I am going to be confident that this is my gift and something that God wants me to do. I do not want to fail or get hurt again. Get rid of that "smh" emoji. I want God to direct my path and be pleased.

True, when you make a mistake, some friends will talk about you and walk away. Others will hang in there with you, but eventually they will get tired. But not God. That is not God's mode of operation. God's DNA is full of everlasting love, patience, brand-new mercies, and grace for us. If you make a mistake, God will give you the strength and the resilience to keep going. God knows that you are not perfect. If you follow His plans, then you will not be destroyed by life's pits and traps. Because you have messed up, people will say terrible things about you. People quickly forget that they have made mistakes too. People will be unforgiving, mistreat you, and make you the next whipping boy. Just know that God can take those same disparaging words and juxtapose the harshness with words that compliment you. God can lift you up in spite of their hurtful and condescending actions made toward you. God can use mistakes meant to tear you down to build you up.

No weapon formed against you will prosper; and every tongue that shall rise against thee in judgment thou shalt condemn. This is the heritage of the servants of the Lord, and their righteousness is of me, saith the Lord" (*Isa. 54:17*).

"For the just man falls seven times; and rises again, but the wicked shall fall into mischief" (*Prov. 24:16*).

From personal experience, you have more than seven times to make a mistake. No, God is not happy because you keep making the same mistakes. Like a parent, God does not rejoice when you are hurt and in pain. But guess what, you do not have to keep making those same mistakes. God has a plan to help us if we wait on Him. Newsflash—God does not want us to be in a bondage mold when we make mistakes. Instead acknowledge the mistake and seek God for guidance and strength to avoid the pitfalls. As you begin trusting God, you will learn how to avoid those stumbling blocks. Then God will use you to help others to avoid the same obstacles. You have not forgotten the endured callous mistreatment of others, the toxic relationships, or the wrong choices made on your part.

That is why you are the right person to help others and tell them what to look out for. You are an expert in dealing with the opportunistic chameleons that pretend to look out for you. With each episode, you tell yourself that this is the last time that you are going to fall for that trap

> *Life Point # 8*
>
> *While forgiving others, do not forget to forgive yourself so you can be free to move on. Do not allow unforgiveness to hinder or stunt your growth.*

or believe that person. Instead of bulletproofing your feelings in preparation for the next hurt or mistake, ask God to reassure and encourage your heart. Ask God for clarity and discernment to be more decisive. Forgive yourself and others. One recommendation after forgiveness is to use those incidents as life learning lessons to avoid hurt in the future.

Stop focusing on your mistakes. God certainly isn't. He is looking at what you can become. You still have a chance to get things right. Focus on the fact that you still have a chance to do God's work. You still have time to turn your life around with the help of God. God is changing you from glory to glory. Remember you are not perfect and never will be. It is through Christ that we are perfected. The good news is that God still loves you and stands ready willing and able to help you fulfill your purpose. God knows about every mistake. He has forgiven you and wants to propel you forward.

Reason 5 I Can Take Care of This by Myself

Really! How is that working for you? Are you satisfied with the results? John 15:5 says that you can do nothing without God. The truth is that you cannot do anything that is going to get you the kind of creditable results that you will need to sustain complete success and total victory. Besides, you do not have to handle or do everything by yourself. God did not create you to be Superman or one of the Avengers. You do not have to wear that cape. You have no supernatural abilities. God does not want you to walk around thinking that you are She-Hulk or some other superhero. So, whatever you need to do, you do not have to do it by yourself.

Many times, we take on the burden of others. We feel like no one else is going to do it, so we rush in and immediately try to fix stuff. We quickly find that the burden is unbearable and often become frustrated and eventually resentful. We are trying to help other people with their issues, and we can barely keep our own affairs straight.

We are trying to take on assignments that we are ill equipped to cope with. Although you took some courses in a church or civilian counseling program, you are still not equipped to deal with people's childhood trauma and adulthood drama. By the time you address their baggage, you will feel beat up and used. You will question why you feel this way since you were doing a work for the Lord. But you were doing the work for the Lord without Him. You were doing the work with your strength, instead of His.

Before we can change anything, we need God to work in us and through us. We were not created to fix or solve everybody's problems. We must realize that there are some things that God will give us the wisdom and the strength to fix, and there are some things that God will choose to fix later in that person's life. Often, God is allowing their situation to get their attention so that they will trust Him. Have you considered that God may want to use someone else instead of you to rectify the situation? Have you actively sought the Lord's direction concerning your role in the life of the person who you are trying to help?

I finally realized that during those times, I need to ask myself, "Did God give me that assignment?" I was so beat down that I was running around saying things like "unless God is at the door, don't answer it." Then, I had the audacity to say that "If God is at the door, then He had better give me a sign."

Life Point # 9

At times, we are our worst enemy! Lord, rescue me from myself!
(Psalm 39:7-8)

Teach me to depend on You and not my emotions and limited skills. Help me to redeem my time wisely.

> **Life Point # 10**
>
> *When you establish a negative codependent relationship with another, you are robbing yourself and them of the opportunity to experience God-trusting and God-responding moments. Turn your desire to help and their desire to receive help over to God. Give God time to work things out.*

That is awful! What happened to me! What happened to "God, You are welcome in this place!"? I will tell you what happened. I put myself along with my rescue cape in the space where God should have been. Theoretically, I was helping people with my limited strength and ability. I was depending on me to help others make positive changes in their life.

Have you been there? I hope not, but maybe you have felt that way. Chances are, we took it upon ourselves to rescue others. I will admit that I wore that badge and tee shirt. We absolutely cannot be the savior for others. There is only one Savior, and He is Jesus Christ, the Son of God. We cannot allow people to become codependent. That is draining and, overall, it does not help anyone. Codependency does not build up relationships. Instead, it demolishes relationships. We must pray for others and convince them to trust God in their situation. Whatever you need, God can do it. God can supply it. We can only do things through Christ.

"I can do all things through Christ who strengthens me" (*Phil. 4:13*) **(NKJV).**

I learned that I get weary, impatient, perplexed, disappointed, and sometimes angry when I use my own strength to manage things. God does not want you to faint. He does not want you to become angry and bitter. God does not want you to get off track.

Hindsight dictates that I should have prayed first about the situation. There is certainly nothing wrong with taking the time out to pray. Just tell that person requesting your assistance to hold that thought. The situation always looks different after prayer. Ask God first if He wants you to do the thing that you are about to do. No matter how noble the task is, if God did not assign that mission to you, you have to say no. Remember, you can still pray for them. If God assigned that mission to you, then He will let you know.

The money I could have saved if I had prayed first. I used to be a sucker for sad stories. The husband of one of my good friends told me that they were about to be evicted. He explained that he had not been able to pay the rent for the last three months. He said that he would repay the money. I started thinking about my friend and their kids. I started thinking about my family and how I would feel if I were about to be evicted. I donned the cape. I produced the money so that they would not have to leave their home. After I gave him the money, I still did not take off the cape. I started thinking that if they did not have the money to stay in their home, then they might not have the money to purchase food. I did not want their kids to starve. So up, up, and away I went to the commissary to purchase groceries. Well, I found out later from my friend that they did not need help with the rent. The husband had already talked to the property owner about collaborating with him to repair and repaint his other properties. Instead of monetarily paying him for his help, the property owner would deduct his back rent. In other words, the problem had already been resolved. She was grateful for the groceries, but they had that covered too. She apologized for her husband's deceit and promised that they would repay the money.

That incident occurred many years ago, and they have not repaid the money. They made one attempt to pay the money about three or four years after the incident. We have not heard from them since. Bottomline, I bought into a need based on deception. I thought that I could manage the situation myself. I should have consulted God first. My husband and I should have waited a few more days to continue praying about the situation. That extra time would have certainly allowed us to check out the situation. We would have had the time to find additional resources for them and to get spiritual guidance from our pastor. We should have waited to receive an answer from God. Nevertheless, I was deceived into believing a lie and thinking that I could help solve their predicament.

Joshua was deceived by the Gibeonites. The Gibeonites lied about where they came from. They pretended that they had come from a faraway land when they were from a neighboring tribe. The Gibeonites knew that God had given the land to the Israelites, and they did not want to be destroyed. The Gibeonite leaders disguised themselves as weary travelers from a distant land. They asked Joshua to make a covenant with them. The covenant guaranteed that the Israelites would not attack the Gibeonites. Joshua did not consult the Lord. Three days later, he discovered the truth about the Gibeonites (Josh 9:3–18).

Unfortunately, that is not the only incident that I thought that I had the solution to solving the problem. I put on the cape and jumped into action more times than I am willing to admit. Ready, cue music. I had to learn that if God does not give you that assignment, then it is best if you do not accept it. I learned how to pray for individuals and help them find free resources that will meet their need.

Life Point # 11

Encourage yourself and others to wait quietly before the Lord. Your victory, help, strength, and reassurance comes from God (Psalm 62:1-3).

I discovered that if God wants you to help and bless others, then He will give you the wisdom, discernment, strength, resources, and the endurance to hang in there until the problem is resolved or God sends relief. If God wants you to get involved with helping others beyond prayer and pointing out resources, He will let you know. When God wants you to help others, He will make the burden light and assist while you help. God will send others to share in the burden. You will not feel alone or compelled to take on more than you can handle. Sometimes, your job is just to pray and offer words of encouragement. How about smiling, a gentle hug, or kindness? Before you take it too far (do not put on the cape) and start feeling like you can contend with everything by yourself, wait on the Lord for His direction.

Reason 6 Other People Know What to Do

There are experts out there, who specialize in various areas that render their services helpful. They can instruct and answer questions. They get paid big bucks to make a positive difference in your life. Even though, they may provide excellent advice, you still need to pray and ask God for His guidance.

God created experts in every field, but they do not know everything. They certainly do not know more than God. It does not matter if they have a doctorate degree in a certain area. Someone once said that a PhD without God stands for "poor helpless dummy" or "powerless hysterical dunce." Experts understand and have knowledge in their field of study. I taught English and reading for over twenty years. Please do not ask me anything about statistics. You will get the wrong answer. Because God knows everything, He is your best bet for the right solution. Only God knows your future and the right path for you. Hebrews 12:2 says that God is the author and the finisher of our faith.

Even if other people know what is going on with you right now, they still cannot see into your future. They cannot predict everything that is going to happen to you. Only God has absolute insight. Yes, people and doctors can tell you that if you do not stop drinking, lose weight, change your diet, or take certain medication, you might die from a stroke or a heart attack. But they are speaking in terms of scientific or medical data. They are talking in generalities. They do not have a crystal ball that shows them specifically what is going to happen to you or where you will be in the future.

There is nothing wrong with consulting or looking to professionals for their medical, educational, legal, artistic, or technical advice. That is what they get paid for. God is not insecure. He already knows that no one can take His place or do His job. These doctors cannot move mountains, tear down walls, or deliver people out of the lion's den. They do not get paid to perform miracles. And any miracle that happens is because God is working through them.

Even though they offer medical information and advice, we must realize that these experts are human, and much of their knowledge comes from their academic and occupational experiences. Their knowledge is finite. God's knowledge is infinite.

The experts, based on their expertise and data, make decisions, or offer their best estimates. Sometimes their decisions deliver the desired response, and sometimes they do not. God knows everything and has the final say. God's decisions always produce the best results. Unlike a car mechanic, God does not have to run a series of tests to tell you what He thinks is wrong. God does not have to consult anyone else before making His diagnosis. God does not have to put you in a shop for a week, waiting for parts and more opinions. God does not even charge you for labor. God identifies the problem instantly and already has the remedy.

Your best bet is to pray for the people that you have chosen to give you advice and are collaborating with you. Tell God thank you for bringing those experts in your life to help you. Pray that God will guide them in the operating room, court room, classroom, in your business, and so forth. Although you are grateful for the experts, keep your trust in God.

Reason 7 My Friends Criticize Me for Not Doing What They Say

Friends can often be harsh and supercritical when they want you to follow their lead. They will question why you are choosing to wait on God, especially when they are not able to see acceptable or immediate results. We often find ourselves doing what they say so we will not be ostracized.

Not Willing to Wait

Unfortunately, friends can be very fickle. No sooner than you do what they have told you to do, they often change their position. As soon as you confront and remind them that they initially agreed with the decision, they will say that you misunderstood. They will simply find a way to point the problem back to you. It becomes your fault that you have this problem.

Sometimes they throw the outcome in your face. Especially when the outcome produces negative results. No one wants to take credit when things backfire. Don't you just hate it when people say, "You should have known better than to do that!" or "If it had been me, I would have n-e-v-e-r done that!" As if those excuses give them the right to back pedal and disavow their part in the situation.

Just dig the dagger in deeper. They will never admit that it was their advice that you were following in the first place. They will disavow any knowledge on their part. They suddenly get amnesia and refuse to acknowledge how their criticism and misjudgment pressured you into making certain decisions. That is right! You were just trying to appease them, and now look at the mess.

Obviously, if the outcome yields positive results, they will take the credit. They will rub the "I told you so" in your face more times than you care to look at their smug smile. They want to ensure that you never question their opinion again while boasting that they are smarter than you. Again, when problems develop, suddenly the people who were initially with you now act like you do not exist. They have already alienated you, and now you are human fodder for anyone who wants to feed off your carcass.

In 1 Kings 18:20, King Ahab gave the order to bring the false prophets together at Mt. Carmel. Elijah killed them there. Once Ahab arrived home in chapter 19:1, he told Jezebel "all that Elijah had done." Nowhere do we find that Ahab shared with his wife that he had called them all together. Ahab more than likely did not admit that he summoned the pagan prophets to Mount Carmel, the place of their demise. He did not convey that his order was the reason that her prophets were there in the first place. Ahab knew his wife and more than likely figured

Life Point # 12

When life's circumstances turn out right, people gladly acknowledge and share their contributions to your success. They smile, wink, nod and give the thumbs up sign. At times, they take too much credit. However, when things go awry, people rarely admit culpability. They will ignore, talk about and leave you to endure the repercussions and most of the burden alone.

out that she would be enraged and violent. He knew that her savagery would not be appeased, and revenge would be her resolution. Now, she may have known because he also summoned the people. But by focusing her attention on what Elijah had done to her prophets, he managed to keep Jezebel's fury on Elijah. While Jezebel was sending a messenger with murderous threats to Elijah, King Ahab ensured that Elijah was the only one who would take the fall.

That is why we need to be in tune with the leadership of the Holy Spirit. God will never trick and deceive people into acting inappropriately. God will always tell you the right things to do and never leave you when problems occur. We must yield to the Holy Spirit as it leads, guides, and directs. God will not point a condemning finger or cast blame on you. Even though your friends may have threatened to kick you to the curb, God will not turn His back on you.

Take the time to seek God for direction. God will not throw things in your face, abandon you, or talk about you. God does not have a false agenda. If your friend's advice does not line up with the Word of God, then you should not do what your friends are telling you to do. If they are loyal friends, then they are not going to sow discord or force you to act ungodly. They will realize that we all have fallen short and need to treat people the way we want to be treated. Genuine friends will want what is best for you, and they will admit that God's way is the right way to solve all problems. They will not put you in compromising positions or ask you to do things that make you uncomfortable. They will not try to control you or be hypocritical. If they are following God's leading, then they will want what is best for you. They will be empathetic and reflective. They would say "If it had not been the Lord who was on our side . . ." (Ps. 124). Recommend that they pray for you.

Reason 8
I Like To Do What Others Do Because If It Worked for Them, Then It Will Work for Me

Not necessarily. Another person's reality or solution may not be a good fit for you. What worked for your friend may or may not work for you. What kept your friend's marriage together may create a hostile environment in your relationship. The study habits of others may have helped them get through high school and college but may do little to get you a passing grade. Now some of their recommendations may be good, but the situations are not one hundred percent identical. Ask yourself these questions and then consider the differences:

- Do you have access to the same or better resources or support systems that helped them?

- Do you know the whole story, and do you share the same goals?

- Are you aware of the other alternatives they considered or the outside factors that led them to make their decision?

- Have you walked in their moccasins, or have they walked in your shoes?

What they advised you to do works up to a certain point. You may find that you can only use one or two methods or ideas that they proposed while discarding the others. Those one or two steps may be the only steps that apply to your personal situation and will help you to achieve your goals.

Many times, things look a lot easier than they really are. People rarely tell you the whole story. They tell you what they want you to hear. They describe their brilliance in catching the fish but omit the part where they bought the wrong bait or fell into the water. They tell you the part of how they got their licensure, but they forgot to mention the sacrifices and how much money was needed to resuscitate their dream. Unless you were there the entire time, you really do not know what is behind their story. Do not be so hasty to do exactly what they are doing or what people tell you to do. Their lifestyle, challenges, aspirations, objectives, and or motivation may not be the same. What they did may not work for you, even if it worked for them. Remember "the grass is not always greener on the other side."

Stop comparing your situation with others. Have you prayed first and asked God what He thinks? Are you chasing after the things of God or trying to live your friend's dreams?

In 1 Samuel 18:5–7, King Saul heard the women singing that "Saul has killed his thousands, and David his ten thousands." Saul became jealous and began to despise David. Why? So what that David killed more men in battle than he did. Weren't they on the same side? Instead of being grateful that he was still alive to hear the song, Saul compared his kill count to David's. He was upset that David's exploits were greater than his.

Saul never stopped to consider that killing more than a thousand was not his mandate. Maybe striking down one thousand was all that he could handle. God will not put more on you than you can bear. God did not give Saul David's assignment. Saul was not supposed to do everything David did. Saul did not kill Goliath. David did (1 Samuel, chapter 17). Saul did not make any comparison then.

You may not be able to do what others do and achieve the same results. God has a tailor-made mission just for you. You are not designed to do what everyone else is doing. Instead, do what God wants you to do.

"Seek you first the kingdom of God and his righteousness, and all these things will be given to you as well" (*Matt. 6:33*).

Ask God to send someone who has wisdom to help you make the best decision for your assignment. If you have found yourself coveting the things that your friend has, repent. Ask God to establish His priorities for you. Do not waste time focusing on what your friends are doing and how good they look and what they have. For all you know, they may be working diligently toward world domination. You may admire their determination and success, but your spiritual goals may be different.

"What does it profit a man to gain the whole world but lose his soul? (*Luke 9:25, Mark 8:36 and Matthew 16:26*).

The key then is to consider what God's will or purpose for your life is. What does God want you to do? Do their recommendations and advice align with God's will? Are they following God's will in their own lives? Are you following them and the things that they do because they are godly or just popular? Do not follow everything social influencers are doing. If God is pleased with what you are doing, then do not worry about pleasing everybody else.

"Do not conform to the pattern of this world but be transformed by the renewing of your mind. Then you will be able to test and approve what God's will is—his good, acceptable, and perfect will" (*Rom. 12:2*).

If you are chasing after the things of God and allowing the Holy Spirit to be your guide, then you will be successful. With God's favor, guidance and peace operating daily in our lives, we will be blessed. Not only will we be blessed, but our future generations as well.

"May the Lord richly bless you and your children" (*Ps. 115:14*).

Reason 9
I Already Know What God Is Going to Do Because God Did the Same Thing the Last Time

No, you do not! There we go again, thinking we know everything that God is going to do. Impossible! We cannot begin to know what God is doing. We do not think or act like God.

Therefore, do not waste time boasting in your abilities. Instead, boast in His grace.

But He said to me , " My grace is sufficient for you, for my power is made perfect in weakness." Therefore I will boast all the more gladly about my weakness." 2nd Cor. 12:9 (NIV)

Never assume that God is going to do the same thing the same way all the time. God does new things in us (Isa. 43:18-19) and for us. God always provides but the method of provision might change. God changes the method to make sure that we will continue to depend on Him. If we know what is going to happen in advance or if we know the way God is going to make things happen, our reliance level will decrease dramatically. That is not what God wants. He wants us to depend on Him rather than someone else. If you think God is going to duplicate the same things every time or the same process for you as He does for your friends and others, then you have already missed the mark.

God's hands are not tied. God heals, but He does not have to heal the same way. The manner of healing is God's choice. God delivers and restores, but He may restore or deliver one person one way and someone else another way. That is why when we pray, we need to pray God's will. Additionally, trust God to be inventive and even reckless if He desires. Tell God that you are excited about what He is going to do. Let him know that if He blessed you like that this last time, you cannot wait for what He is going to do this time. God knows what is best for you. As you grow in faith, God will show you different things.

God does not have to operate in the exact same way all the time. He can change up. You will have to fight some battles, but God will fight with you. For other battles, God will say that you will not have to fight at all. God will do the fighting for you. Jehoshaphat, king of Judah, and his army were in a battle that they did not have to fight. The Ammonites, Moabites, and some of the Meunites were planning to gang up and attack the Israelites. God sent the word that this battle was his (2 Chron. 20:1-25). You know who won.

What a relief to know that sometimes God will have us watch him fight the battle. You do not have to part the Red Sea (Exod. 14: 21-22) or make the sun stand still (Josh. 10:12-14). Let God do it! With God on your side, who can be against you? With God on your side, you are in the majority. So, the prayer question for God should be, "Will you be with me?" You can also ask God "What should I do?" or "What do You want me to do?" If God is with you, then you are going to make it.

"You are the God who performs miracles; you display your power among the peoples" (*Ps. 77:14*) (**NIV**).

God will direct you. God can send the answer directly or through dreams, visions, people, and situations. Remember, God can make a donkey talk if He wants to get your attention (Num. 22:28). You must wait for Him.

The point is that God always knows what is best for us. We must stay in lockstep with Him and not the other way around. We must be in tune so we can know when God makes a change. We do not want to become so presumptuous that we think we know all of God's moves. God may reveal some things, but you will never know everything that God is doing. Truthfully, we cannot imagine or even fathom all the things that God knows or is going to do.

"However, as it is written: 'What no eye has seen, what no ear has heard, and what no human mind has conceived'—the things God has prepared for those who love him" (*1 Cor. 2:9*).

When we think about the power of God, we must be confident that God can do anything but fail. That is not just a song that we sing. God, who is the same yesterday, today, and forevermore is free to change His game plan for us whenever He likes. The only game plan that God will not change for us is His love and His precious gift of salvation.

God knows the situation better than we do. He has already figured out the best course of action to take. God can take as much time as needed. Any reason that we can use as an excuse for not waiting on God is superficial in comparison to the vastness of God's timely provision. God is always prepared in every case. There is no situation that comes as a surprise to Him.

When we fail to wait on God, we will always have that exasperating "Oh My God, what have I done" experience! You know the experience where you jump out the frying pan into the fire. Your impatience will burn you up! We need to consider the big picture before, not after, we act erratically.

How badly do you want to achieve your goals, dreams, requests, or answers? Are you willing to wait on God and stop making vain excuses? Are you willing to wait on God's plans to unfold instead of bulldozing your plans to the forefront. God wants you to know that He is looking out for you and is mindful of everything you need. God wants you to trust Him in all circumstances. Stop doing things your way and wait on God.

Chapter 3

Hurry Up and Wait

(Do Not Prolong the Wait)

Ask any soldier what they remember the most about going to the rifle range or picture day. They will tell you that they had to get up extremely early just to wait around needlessly before the mission could be completed. Someone or something would inevitably cause the unnecessary delay. Hence, the prolonged wait. Let us not even talk about the lost time during the mandatory parade formations.

Soldiers remember arriving at dawn just to wait for about an hour or two before the instructor in charge of the range would get there. God forbid if range control personnel were not available. The range would not open. Sleepy-eyed soldiers longing for more time to sleep were forced out of bunks into an old army cattle car or the back of a deuce and half. Some soldiers did not ride in vehicles. They had to road march. The weapons were transported to the range. Traffic was not a problem at that time in the morning because no one else was on the road. Even physical training (PT) started a little later.

So, you rush to get there before the sun comes up only to wait. Finally, two hours later, everyone is ready to start. Most soldiers had the same thought on their mind. If the unit knew that the event would commence at a certain time, then why was it necessary to be enroute to the range so early. The soldiers agreed that they were rushed to the range just to wait a couple of hours before it opened. They were rushed to the range to end up stuck in a holding pattern. Hence, the term "Hurry up and wait."

It seems like such an extended period goes by after we let our request be known to the Lord. We bark out our commands and then put God on our tight timetable. In a hurry, we rushed out our request, and now we wait. Some jokingly feel that if they would have known that God did not have any intention of granting that request promptly, they could have waited until later to make that request. Was it necessary for God to make us wait on the promise? Does God operate under the concept of "Hurry Up and Wait"?

God is the only one who can answer that. God moves the way He moves. In Him we live, move, and have our being (Acts 17:28), not the other way around. Look, the wait is long enough without placing foolish time demands on God. This is not a sporting event. Put your stopwatch away. The wait is hard enough without weighing it down with impatience, doubt, negativity, and other cynical factors that further prolong the waiting process. Like the Israelites, you will be going around that mountain too many times. The Israelites were close to the Promised Land and still could not go in. Talk about hurrying up and waiting. They were stuck in a holding pattern.

The reason that God has not produced the thing that you have been waiting for is because you are not waiting right. Just because you feel that you have waited a long time does not mean that you have waited in the right manner, with the right attitude and humility. When we start waiting in a manner that pleases God, our answers will come sooner. Here are some hindering factors that weigh you down, prolong the wait, and clog the flow of God's blessings.

Hindering Factor 1 False Pride

God hates pride because it creates a false sense of security in one's own ability. False pride inflates the ego and makes you think that you are better and smarter than everyone else. God is not against confidence, but He detests a boastful and arrogant spirit. False pride will always push you in the wrong direction. It will push you further from reliance and trust in God. False pride leads to a rejection of God's way for self-aggrandizement. False pride coerces you into thinking that your plan is best and must be employed with deliberate activation despite outcomes. False pride will never have you consider consequences, other alternatives, or promote time to wait on God. Instead, false pride advances its own selfish agenda and egotistical appeal. Too much pride interferes with relationships, destroys your ability to discern the truth, and causes you to please others rather than God.

Life Point # 13

Listening to people will often cause you to ignore God's instructions and miss opportunities. Don't listen to what they say. Watch what they do. God always leads the humble in doing right, teaching them His ways. (Psalm 25:8))

"Humble yourselves therefore under the mighty hand of God, that he may lift you up in due season. Cast all your anxiety on him because he cares for you" (*1 Pet. 5:6–7*).

Humble yourselves before you are crushed and humiliated. That is painful and devastating. God does not want that experience for you. However, God will allow it to get you to the place where you are ready to acknowledge that you really do need Him. If you just wait on God, then God will exalt you at the proper time. God is always willing to extend a hand to assist. He watches over us and knows that we cannot make it without Him. He longs to be in a relationship with us and be the solution to the obstacles we encounter.

We have two options in every instance. We can either choose to do things God's way, or we can do the opposite. Many times, we choose the latter. We believe that because of our education, finances, and experience, we know how to take care of things so there is no need to consult the Lord. That is where we mess up. We refuse to release our pride and humble ourselves even when we know that the outcome would be so much better. It is exceedingly difficult for us to admit or apologize when we are wrong. Most of the time we are in complete denial because we cannot accept that we have faults. We tend to blame secondary sources instead of looking in the mirror. Just face it; we do not know everything.

If you are hurting over past traumatic events, tell God about it. You do not have to keep a tight grip on the reigns to compensate or cover up for the shame, guilt, or anger that you might feel. You do not have to remain in a holding pattern, blaming yourself or others. Ask God to help you to release your pride so that you can rely on Him.

Hindering Factor 2 Negative and Stubborn Attitude

People who are always negative and stubborn have a challenging time accepting help or advice from others, even God. They boast about their abilities and rarely show appreciation for anything, or what anybody says or does that fails to recognize their point of view. As far as you are concerned, you are not budging. It is your way or the highway. You ignore or devalue what others have to say, choosing to do things your own way. Even after being proven wrong, you still refuse to budge from your way of thinking or stand down. There's truth to the saying, "If you keep doing things the same way, you will get the same result." Despite this simple truth, you are determined to repeat the same detrimental actions.

You have turned countless people off with your judgmental opinions. You automatically think that people are against you and want you to fail. You put up an impenetrable wall of defense to deliberately keep others out. You see being cooperative or yielding as a sign of weakness. You feel that if you are open or transparent, then people will take advantage. You find it difficult to abandon your convictions and ideas. You feel that if you support others, you will be blamed and left holding the bag.

Have you ever stopped to consider that God has set these people in your path to instruct and assist you? Have you considered that God is trying to soften your hardened heart so that you will be more receptive to the people and things of God? Maybe having the upper hand has not only alienated you from others but from God as well. Maybe your adversity is God's way of chastising you for your obstinance. Stop kicking the boulder and wondering why your foot hurts. God is trying to get your attention. God is breaking that willful spirit to mold you.

"Repent at my rebuke! Then I will pour out my thoughts to you, I will make known to you my teachings" (*Prov. 1:23*) (NIV).

Ask God to soften your heart and help you to be receptive to His will. The pharaoh refused to liberate God's people and look what happened to him. You do not want to be swallowed up by the Red Sea in your life. Ask God to forgive you for anything that you have said or done that bought offense. Do not say, "If I have offended anyone . . ." Stop. You know that you have. Ask God to help you get things right. The truth is that none of us really want to miss all that God has planned. Acknowledge God as the Alpha and the Omega in your life. Let God take the lead.

Hindering Factor 3 Wrong Intent

What is the real reason behind your actions? If you are motivated by your own greed, lust, and love of power, then you are heading down a destructive path. Even if your actions are genuine or good, you still need to ensure that you have the right motivation. What is the right motivation? What makes you behave in a certain way? Your ambition must be God-centered. If your focus is on any other agenda, then the enemy can use it to distract and eventually decimate you. Being off focus causes you to work harder to achieve your goals. Being off track causes you to lose more time. Time is certainly not a commodity that we can afford to waste. Spending too much time focusing on worldly events can be depressing and takes your mind off what God wants you to do. You can become ungrateful and develop a complaining spirit just by watching the news.

"Set your mind on things above, not on earthly things"
(*Col. 3:2*) (NIV).

God does not want you to be deceived by the enemy's traps. Keep your mind on things that motivate and inspire you. Avoid pitching your tent along unfruitful paths. Safeguard your heart and be mindful of worldly influences.

"Keep thy heart with all diligence; for out of it are the issues of life"
(*Prov. 4:23*).

Avoid maintaining negative relationships and trying to please or placate people that encourage your disobedience to God. They are not your friends and are not looking out for what is best for you. Pray for them, but until they change their focus, you need to cut them off. Surround yourself with people who trust God and will encourage you to do the same.

Pray and ask God to transform you by renewing your mind (Rom. 12:2) and fixing your heart. Ask God to help you to see life the way He does so that you will not be disheartened by secular distractions. God will give you the strength to recognize abusers and not conform to their manipulation. Keeping your mind on what pleases the Lord will help you stay focused, grow in grace, and be successful.

"Finally brethren, whatsoever things are true, whatsoever things are honest, whatsoever things are just, whatsoever things are pure, whatsoever things are lovely, whatsoever things are of good report; if there be any virtue, and if there be any praise, think on these things. What soever is lovely think on these things. " (*Phil. 4:8*)

Hindering Factor 4 Not Ready for the Blessing (Rushing)

We often remind my grandson not to rush through his homework. Rushing usually causes him to forget something. He would have to go back to finish it or start over again. We tried to teach him to take his time and take the time to check over his work. We told him that the teacher might not give him the opportunity to redo the assignment. In life, there are no guarantees of redoes. There are consequences for rushing or not following through correctly. In football, if one or more of the defensive players move too soon on the line, the referee will call out the encroachment violation and stop the game. The referee will blow his whistle and throw out the yellow flag. He will call out the player and the penalty. The team is penalized via lost yardage for moving too soon and not waiting for the hiked ball. Often in life, we are penalized for moving too quickly, being unprepared, or being in the wrong position.

Sometimes when we rush through life, we do not develop the tools needed for success at the next level. We are dangerous when we lack maturity or are not ready for the assignment. When we are not ready, we complicate things. Why are you asking God to send you a godly man or woman when you are not ready to be faithful? Although, God desires to bless you, He does not want to give you something that you cannot handle. Why should God move on your behalf if you are not ready to do your part. When we try to rush the blessing, we fail to learn the importance of commitment, appreciation, responsibility, and tolerance of others. We lack stick-to-itiveness. God wants us to keep on going, but we want to quit and give up. God wants us to change, but we are still wallowing in the mud.

God wants us to be successful, but we must be ready. When we lack moral character and integrity, God will take the time needed to develop our character. God wants us to be in the right position to receive the blessing. When we are not ready to receive a requested prayer, we are ungrateful, take advantage, and mistreat others. We become opportunists and feel entitled. God knows that if your integrity and character are questionable, then the enemy has a foothold. How are you representative of godly character when you are doing everything that the world is doing?

"In all things show yourself to be an example of good deed, with purity in doctrine, dignified, sound in speech is beyond reproach, so that the opponent will be put to shame, having nothing bad to say about us" (*Titus 2:7–8*).

Lack of character is one of the reasons God does not make haste with some of our requests. We need more character-building time so as not to bring a reproach on ourselves and others. It is hard to preach to others about positive lifestyle changes when you know in your heart that you are still singing the same tune. God wants to see a renewing change in you. God does not want to put more on you than you can tolerate. God will not put or keep you in a position of power if your goal is to hurt and abuse people. God does not want you to house hatred and hostility in your heart. God wants you to turn those character weaknesses over to Him. The Holy Spirit is the character builder. He will speak to your heart and give you the strength to take corrective actions.

When God does not deliver when we think He should, we become angry and question God. We are upset with God because we think we are ready for the blessing that He has yet to grant. What is the holdup? We think that no more time is necessary, and we are ready to proceed. We do not realize that we are like the slimy caterpillar going through the full process of metamorphosis before transforming into a beautiful butterfly. We are like the homely duckling before it turns into a graceful swan. It takes time for us to grow in grace and mature in the Lord. When we are fearful and doubt God, God takes the time to reshape us. God does not want us to limit what He is trying to do for us and through us.

God is righteous and just. He will never give us more than we can take care of. His plan is not designed to hurt or destroy us. God's plan equips and prepares us for the work that He wants us to do. God will not elevate us too soon. We might hurt ourselves and others. God wants us to persevere successfully.

"And thou shalt remember all the way which the Lord thy God led thee these forty years in the wilderness, to humble thee, and to prove thee, to know what was in thine heart, whether thou would keep his commandments, or no" (*Deut. 8:2-5*).

God will take the time needed to prepare us for the journey. God wants us ready to fulfill the plan that He has for us. God wants to use us for kingdom building. Your life is not about what you want and when you want it. The sooner we realize that the sooner we will be on our way to finding joy, peace, and contentment in our situation.

Hindering Factor 5 Unbelief

You must believe that God is able to do all things. God cannot fail or lie. He orders your steps flawlessly as He establishes His plans for you. You must believe that God has designed the best plans for you. You must believe that God is able to bless you and turn things around. Once you make your request known, you must utilize your faith to trust God and believe that He will bring your request to fruition. Even though we know that we should trust and believe God, we would rather believe everybody else. We will turn everywhere and spend money on everything before we accept the fact that God is the answer. We will call everybody else before we take the time to pray and consult God.

We tend to go to God after everything else has failed. We do not believe that God is going to fulfill His promise.

No matter how difficult or how long the wait, never doubt God. God is a prayer-answering God. God wants us to have faith that He will perform what He has promised. When things do not happen as expected, do not think God is slack or unable to deliver. It simply may mean that God has something else in store for you. It may mean that God is taking the time to make all the necessary changes in you and others to manifest the thing that you desire. You need to endure the waiting process to discover God's purpose and plan. Even though man may have been faulty in delivering what he has promised, God is never faulty. Keep your faith in God.

"And without faith it is impossible to please him: for he that cometh to God must believe that he is, and that he is a rewarder of them that diligently seek him" (*Heb. 11:6*).

Start thanking God in advance for what He is going to do. God has already changed things for you. God has already performed miracles on your behalf. Never forget about what He has already done for you and others. As you progress in your commitment to God, God will increase your responsibility or help you to operate at that level of authority. Remember "to whom much is given, much is required" (Luke 12:48). Do not let unbelief, dissatisfaction, and doubt rob and fill you with regrets over missed opportunities. God has opportunities personally labeled for you and will assign them when He determines that you are ready.

Hindering Factor 6 Anger

Anger is an emotion that we use to express how we feel. Anger can provide positive energy that fuels our support of political, social, and other platforms. When channeled correctly, anger is often the impetus or motivation behind people's reasoning for supporting certain causes or acting in a certain way. When we allow the Holy Spirit to help us use our anger to stand up against the evil acts of the enemy, we can be lighting rods for God. We can use our anger to compel others to action in tearing down strongholds and uplifting godly principles.

Unfortunately, anger is also a negative emotion that causes a root of bitterness and destruction. Anger can cause us to lose perspective, decimate relationships, and take our focus off God. When we feel angry, we must turn to God and trust him to fix the situation. God is the only one who can get to the root cause of our anger. God will not only expose the cause, but He will fill the void in your life with peace and wholeness. God does not want us to use our anger for evil.

"Let all bitterness and wrath and anger and slander be put away from you, with all malice" (*Eph. 4:31*).

The Bible admonishes us to put away all anger and wrath. Anger robs us of our ability to rationally relate to others. Anger causes us to take retaliatory measures to physically hurt or slander others. We must trust God to help us to identify the issues that affect us and cause us to act out of rage. The Holy Spirit can strengthen us to deal with difficult problems and people. The Holy Spirit will move us to a place of discovery and forgiveness. We must deal with anger because it affects our relationship with God and others. Anger hinders our spiritual growth. God will help us to deal with that hurt so that we do not arbitrarily hurt others and make situations worse.

"Be angry, and sin not . . . let not the sun go down upon your wrath" (*Eph. 4:26*).

With God's help, we will not have to do and say things out of anger and then wonder why our situations and relationships have not changed. God wants to move on our behalf, but acting out of anger often hinders our waiting process. God is the only one who can heal the anger because of a traumatic past. God can help us show compassion and extend mercy to others.

Hindering Factor 7 Unforgiveness

It is easy to shut down when we are hurt by others. Depending on the situation, we can hold on to that hurt for years. Unforgiveness robs us of our peace and joy. We are constantly focusing on the words that were haphazardly spoken while replaying the horrid scenario in our heads. We can quote verbatim what was said. We can play back the tone and the facial gestures. With vivid retention, we can recall the pain like it was yesterday. It is hard to let go. But we must release the responsible party as well as ourselves from unfortunate circumstances.

Unforgiveness blocks spiritual blessings and prevents building healthy relationships. It is hard to enjoy and appreciate others when your focus is still on the past and those that have caused the hurt. Unforgiveness will keep you stuck in a holding pattern. Unforgiveness dictates hostility and causes you to act defensively. God is telling you to forgive and show grace and love; yet you have stored up defense mechanisms. God says, "Trust me to direct the situation;" instead, you reinforce your heart and mind with painful memories. Unforgiveness, like anger, poisons you and suppresses your spiritual growth. Unforgiveness gives the offender power over you and cultivates anxiety and bitterness. Anxiety stirs up fear and insecurity while bitterness hardens your heart. Anxiety and bitterness dampen your spirit.

Life Point # 14

When God forgives, He forgets and wipes the slate clean. God does not hold grudges or hold you captive with lingering repetitive reminders. God will help you to start again.

God is not telling you to forget what happened. He is just advising you to trust Him for healing and the power to let go of the people who have hurt you. God wants you to forgive. Remember that God forgave you. If you forgive others who have sinned against you, your heavenly Father will forgive you (Matt. 6:14).

"Bear with one another and forgive one another if any of you has a grievance against someone. Forgive as the Lord forgave you" (*Col. 3:13*) **(NIV).**

God wants to move freely through you and give you a victorious testimony. Unforgiveness hinders your spiritual growth and is an obstacle in your relationship with God.

Hindering Factor 8 Failed to Pass the Test

Think back to the time you were a student in school. When you failed a test, you would receive a lower grade that would negatively affect your overall average. The same applies as we are trying to grow spiritually. Life deals with a series of tests that we must pass before we can move forward. Like the game of chess, certain moves will either take you forward or move you back. If we do not pass the test, we will move back.

The good news is that if we do not pass a test in life, we get to take it again. You have received a bad grade in patience. Do not worry because that test in patience is coming around again. Hopefully, the next time you will recognize early what you need to do. When you pass the test, then you will be able to move forward. Because you pass the test on patience this time, there are no guarantees that you are going to pass this test on patience or any other test each time the test comes around.

We must learn from our mistakes, so we do not have to keep retaking the same test. We can even learn from other people's mistakes. I do not have to see you fall down the steps to learn to hold on to the banister. I can learn how to maneuver the steps by carefully observing you.

Do you need help in loving the unlovable or someone who has hurt you? Do you need help in restoring peace in your life and the lives of others? We always need help from the Holy Spirit to pass each test in life. When we do not wait on the Lord, we either fail the test, or we do not score as high as we would have scored had we waited on God. A teacher has the test key which provides the correct answers. Waiting on God gives us the teacher's key with all the correct answers.

Do you want to know the best way to make it out of the maze? God has the map. He is better than Map Quest and Alexa. You need God's help in life. God never said that you would not have any test. God promises that He would be with you and help you through the trials and tests.

"Consider it an opportunity for great joy when trouble comes your way. For you know that your endurance has a chance to grow when your faith is tested. So let your endurance grow. For when your endurance is fully developed, you will be perfect, and complete, needing nothing" (James 1:2-4).

God wants to validate and affirm you as He successfully moves you through each point on your life's map. God does not want you to fail life's test. God did not promise that you would get through your test or your life's map unscathed. You may have some bumps or bruises, but you will get through stronger and have better test results with Him than without Him. God wants you to pass life's test so that He can promote you for His glory.

Hindering Factor 9 Too Much Baggage Hurt

When we refuse to give God our hurt, we transport that hurt from one destination to another. It does not matter if that hurt is based on our own insecurities, paranoia, shame, guilt, or control issues. It does not matter if that hurt is caused by family, friends, or others. Ironically, we wear that hurt like a badge of honor. We move from one situation, job, school, church, or relationship with that same hurt on display. We tried off-loading the baggage, but something always happens that brings us back to the same place. We know God can help, but we refuse to turn things over to Him. We do not want to give God that bag. Sometimes we even believe that God will help others with their baggage but will not help us. We hold on to the baggage, hoping that things improve. But things do not get better.

The keys that will break that lock on the baggage are grace, empathy, and forgiveness. We must ask God to help us to see and love the person from God's perspective. God sees the inner person and situation exactly how it is. God is the only one who can comfort and restore our broken heart. We put people on a pedestal that only God deserves. We have given people power and control over us so that when we feel mistreated and expectations are not met, we crumble. We expect the people close to us to love and care for us. We expect that they will always treat us right. We can accept society's dysfunction, but there are certain people and situations which we just did not predict would switch from Dr. Jekyll to Mr. Hyde. Now we are in bondage and disillusioned. We do not understand how that person we trusted could cause so much hurt. We feel betrayed. We prayed, but that heavy weight has not moved. The enemy wants to deposit more lies and confusion to seal your bag of hopelessness and steal your freedom. You yearn for acceptance, but that baggage keeps you ostracized and trapped.

"The thief cometh not, but for to steal, and to kill, and to destroy: I am come that they might have life, and that they might have it more abundantly: (*John 10:10*).

God does not want us to live in the shadow of bondage. God wants you to turn that baggage over to Him and move forward. God will help you to forgive and demonstrate godly love. God will even help you to forgive yourself. Somehow, your expectations were impossible for man to meet. Humans are imperfect. Humans will hurt and mistreat you. That is their nature. No one should depend on another person to make them feel secure. God is the only one on whom you should depend.

When you enter a relationship with someone, your trust must remain in the Lord. When you take your focus off God, you are going to be disappointed. When you take your focus off God, the standard drops. Do not expect people to enhance your life because they use idle words. Instead, focus on how they pour into and enrich your life. Whether someone poured a flowing cascade of knowledge, quality mentorship, and opportunity into your life or just a drop, you still must rely on God. God loves you and you are still important to Him. Talk to God about your fears and pain. He will strengthen you and help you to use your experiences with others to propel you forward. You are not defined by the baggage. You are who God says that you are. Your baggage will keep you drowning in the adulation whirlpool.

> *Life Point # 15*
>
> *"If you live for praise, you'll die from rejection." Pastor Eric Moore, Summit Worship Center, Austin, Texas.*
>
> *Do not rely on man to validate you. Your purpose and success has already been designed by God.*

"Be strong and of good courage, do not fear or be afraid of them; for the Lord your God, He is the one who goes with you. He will never leave you or forsake you" (*Deut. 31:6*). (NKJV)

Pray and read the Bible. Listen to sermons and music emphasizing God's unparalleled love and compassion. God's Word always brings peace and clarity. God speaks through His Word and will comfort your broken heart. God will help you to release that baggage and move beyond the hurt. God will help you to forgive people and the painful situations of your past. Worship the Lord and tell Him how much you love and need Him. Affirm God and thank Him for who He is and what He has done. Just like you take the time to acknowledge God, He will affirm you too.

"He heals the brokenhearted and binds up their wounds" (*Ps. 147:3*) **(NIV).**

If you wait on God, He will heal, deliver, and fix things for you. As God is transforming you, He is working on your situation. God is changing things and turning your situation around. What the enemy meant for evil, God meant it for good (Gen. 50:20). He knows how to change perceptions and exalt you at the same time. He can make your enemy your footstool (Heb. 1:13). God will help you use the hurts of your struggle to edify and equip others for their journey.

Hindering Factor 10 Sin

God loves the sinner but hates the sin. It does not matter if the sin is pride, lust, greed, gluttony, envy, or adultery. Sin blocks our blessing and relationship with God. It prevents our prayers and slows our spiritual progress. You are waiting on the Lord to answer prayers, and God is waiting on you to confess the sin in your life.

"If we confess our sins, he is faithful and just and will forgive us our sins and cleanse us from all unrighteousness" (*1 John 1:9*).

Sin creates a big mess and wreaks havoc in our lives. Unconfessed sin is impossible for you to fix because it will not go away. Without the blood of Jesus to wash it clean, sin is a permanent stain. You think you will be able to hide the sin. You will not. You cannot push sin in the closet, shut the door, and pretend that the mess you have created is not there. The only way to deal with sin is through sincere confession to God with repentance.

All these factors block us from receiving our requested prayer and make the wait longer. These hindering factors prevent us from growing. We must repent and turn these factors over to the Lord. We cannot allow these factors to stop our blessings. With God's forgiveness, we can avoid the egg-in-the-face and foot-in-the-mouth degrading moments. When you turn your problems over to God, you do not have to worry about acting inappropriately or looking foolish. When you turn your problems over to God, you do not have to waste time, rush outcomes, and grieve or reminisce about the "I could have", "I would have", and "I should have" moments.

Trust in the Lord with all thine heart, and lean not to your own understanding. In all your ways acknowledge him, and he shall direct thy paths (*Prov. 3:5–6*).

Remember, God can fix everything and give you a fresh start. God wants to restore you and build relationship. Let's maintain a right fellowship with God.

Chapter 4

God Is in the Wait

One of the best reasons for waiting on God is the fact that you do not have to wait alone. God will not leave you in times of adversity. He is not afraid of your circumstances. God is with you on the battlefield and in the lion's den. God did not leave the three Hebrew boys because the fire was too hot. God stepped into the fiery furnace to be with them (Daniel 3:13–25). While you are waiting for your victory, God is standing there to help you through your test.

God is right there by your side, gently coaxing you along. God is like your personal trainer. God knows what exercises are needed to get you in shape and to the finish line successfully. He always designs the best plans for you. He can turn your ashes into beauty (Isa. 61:3).

Years ago, I bought a Tony Little exercise tape. Tony Little is an expert weight trainer and fitness guru. It was shortly after having my third child, and I sorely needed help in losing about thirty-five pounds. Tony knew just the right core exercises to do and never left me alone to do the exercise by myself. He always exercised with me. He would tell me the number of repetitions, so I knew what to expect. He would also explain the benefits of the exercise. Yes, no matter how bad my body hurt, there were benefits. After he introduced the correct way to do the exercise and before he would begin the routine, he would yell out, "*YOU CAN DO IT!*" As you are going through your test, waiting for the miracle or the answered prayer, God is right there with you confirming the same good news: "YOU CAN DO IT!"

As we wait, we need to reflect on who God is, based on His Word and what He has already done. We make our request, and then we spend our time laser-focused on that request and the time that God takes to manifest the desired prayer. Instead of spending the wait time affirming God and building relationship, our prayer life becomes one big visit to God's commissary. Our prayer consisted of "Bless me and mine" and "Gimme," "Gimme," "Gimme" statements.

When this happens, it looks like we are only interested in what we can receive from God, rather than what we can give or offer to God. Therefore, instead of spending extra time on the request, we need to tell God what He means to us. Let God know how much you appreciate that He is in the wait with you. Let God know that you trust Him, and because of Him, you have the confidence to wait. Let God know that you are determined to wait for as long as the Lord deems necessary. There is no time limit or ultimatum. And even if He does not do it, he is still the God of your life.

Here are some principles about God and points we should reflect on as we wait.

Reflection Point 1—The burden that you are trying to carry is too heavy for you. God can carry the weight.

The reality of life dictates that we will experience times on top of the mountain and times when we are in the valley. Life has its ebbs and flows. It is easier to thank God in the good times than it is to thank him when we are going through the turmoil. Despite the obstacles, we must esteem God during the struggle. Despite the pain and sheer gravity of our situations, God helps us to get through it. God is the "how" that gets us through.

Tell God that you will wait because there is no one else who can carry the weight of your burdens. Let God know that He is more than enough, and He controls all things. The poem entitled "*Footprints in the Sand* "by Mary Fishback Powers sums up God's ability to carry our burdens perfectly:

One night I dreamed a dream.
As I was walking along the beach with my Lord.
Across the dark sky flashed scenes from my life.
For each scene, I noticed two sets of footprints in the sand,
One belonging to me and one to my Lord.

After the last scene of my life flashed before me,
I looked back at the footprints in the sand.
I noticed that at many times along the path of my life,
especially at the very lowest and saddest times,
there was only one set of footprints.

This really troubled me, so I asked the Lord about it.
"Lord, you said once I decided to follow you,
You would walk with me all the way.
But I noticed that during the saddest and most troublesome
    times of my life,
there was only one set of footprints.
I don't understand why, when I needed You the most, You would
    leave me." He whispered, "My precious child, I love you and will
    never leave you
Never, ever, during your trials and testings.
When you saw only one set of footprints,
It was then that I carried you."

    This poem is about two sets of footprints in the sand. Two sets of footprints reveal your footprints in the sand and God's footprints walking beside you. One set of footprints illustrates the times God was carrying you. When the weight of life becomes too heavy for you, God picks you up. God is still in the midst, even when you do not see or feel

Him. God wants us to cast our cares on Him. He is always with us. God wants us to give Him our burdens so that He can make the way lighter. We do not have to trudge through the thickets of life, God wants to help us through our difficulties.

"Cast your burden on the Lord, and He will sustain you; He will never allow the righteous to be moved" (*Ps. 55:22*).

"The Lord God is in your midst, a mighty one who will save; he will rejoice over you with gladness; he will quiet you by his love; he will exult over you with loud singing" (*Zeph. 3:17*).

Reflection Point 2 God loves and cares for you!

God does not want you to worry. He comforts and sends angels to protect us. His love is forever, and He goes far beyond our expectations in His favor toward us. When God blesses you, He does not expect payment. Besides, you are unable to pay God. He does not spend time reminding you how many times He has had to help or forgive you. God is for you and is always on your side. God will not run away from you when the crisis becomes overwhelming. God holds your hand and walks you step-by-step through hardships. You can face your battles with God's strength and an awareness that God can conquer any obstacle that you are facing. God does not let go of your hand in fear because the enemy wrongfully boasts and lies. God always loves us, and His love is forever. God will not stop caring for us.

"Give thanks to the Lord, for he is good; his love endures forever" (*1 Chron. 16:34*). **(NIV)**

Reflection Point 3 God knows more than we do.

God knows everything. God knows what is going to happen before it happens. He knows the future. We barely know all the details of the past. There is no shocking or surprising God. He does not have to figure out what the next steps should be. He already knows what to do. You may live by a decision matrix, but God holds the master plan. He is omniscient. God knows the profound and secret things. You cannot hide anything from Him. God already knows what you need. God does not need a therapist to analyze your situation. God does not need a teacher to provide instruction. God does not have any questions that He needs you to answer. If God does asks you a question, it's rhetorical. He is a counselor and a teacher. God's been around since the beginning of time. God created the universe without your geographical advice and offering. There is nothing you can tell Him that He does not already know. Remember, your intelligence is no match with the knowledge of God, and He has the final say.

"Even before there is a word on my tongue, Behold, O Lord, you know it all" (*Ps. 139:4*) (*ESV*).

"Hearken unto this, O Job: stand still, and consider the wonderous works of God. Doest thou know when God disposed them, and caused the light of his cloud to shine? Doest thou know the balancing of the clouds, the wonderous works of him which is perfect in knowledge?" (*Job 37:14–16*).

Reflection Point 4 God is faithful and keeps his promises.

God always keeps His promises. In the Bible, every time the covenant was broken, God was not the culprit. You can stand on the promises of God. God will fulfill His Word and back up what He says. That is why we can walk by faith. He is the unseen variable that makes things happen. We automatically know that God will do what He says. Man may falter on his promises, but God always produces. He hastens to perform His Word. The Lord's Word is dependable and will achieve his intentions (Isa. 55:11).

"For I am the Lord: I will speak, and the word that I shall speak come to pass; it shall be no more prolonged: for in you days, O rebellious house, will I say the word, and will perform it, saith the Lord God" (*Ezek. 12:25*).

"Because of the Lord's great love we are not consumed, for his compassions never fail. They are new every morning; great is your faithfulness" (*Lam. 3:22-23*).

Reflection Point 5 God wants to be involved in our lives.

God calls us friends. A friend is someone who knows you better than most. A friend is someone who you spend quality time with and have formed a special bond with. Many of us have formed bonds that have unfortunately been severed for assorted reasons. God is a faithful friend and will not break His bond with us. He always looks out for us. He blesses us so that we can be a blessing to others.

"I no longer call you servants, because a servant does not know his master's business. Instead, I have called you friends, for everything that I learned from my father I have made known to you" (*John 15:15*) (NIV).

God cherishes the time that we spend with Him. He yearns to communicate with us. He wants us to grow strong in Him so that we can avoid the traps and snares of the enemy. He stands ready, willing, and able to expose the enemy and guide us to the path of righteousness. He embraces us and wants to meet our needs according to His riches in glory. God is there during the times of celebration and the times we are lonely and heartbroken.

"Fear not for I am with you; be not dismayed for I am your God; I will strengthen you; I will help you; I will uphold you with my righteous right hand" (*Isa. 41:10*).

Reflection Point 6 God knows us!

God knows us better than we know ourselves. God knew us before our parents did. God gets us. He understands where we are and knows how to meet us on that level. God knows who takes refuge in Him. God wants to deliver us, but we need to be real with Him. Drop all false pretenses. You cannot fake the funk with God. God knows the number of hairs on your head. King David said that God remembers our tears and collects them in a bottle (Ps. 56:8). God knows intimate details about us. We should be extremely grateful for God's cleansing and saving power. He knows where we came from and where we are going. We cannot fool God with our words and deceptive ploys. He sees our hearts and recognizes who we are in Him.

"But now, this is what the Lord says- he who created you, Jacob, he who formed you, Israel; 'Do not fear, for I have redeemed you; I have summoned you by name; you are mine'" (*Isa. 43:1*) (**NIV**).

Reflection Point 7 God's Plan is the best solution.

God's plans give us a hope and a future. God's plans are sure. We do not see all the hidden traps, but God does. God does not set us up for failure. God loves us so much that He will often close certain doors to us. These doors will often cause us harm, lead us astray, or prevent us from trusting God. Many times, we have asked God to give us things that we really should not have asked for. Later, we learn and understand that God was trying to protect us. Sometimes, we ask God to spare us from certain tests that God could use to elevate us. Instead of demanding that God's shut door be opened, or an opened door be shut, we need to trust God. Try thanking him for shutting that door and start rejoicing for the door that He is getting ready to open. Thank Him for every door that was a part of His plan. That door led to an experience that made you stronger and wiser. God does not want to see us hurt and knows what the best course of action is. For every door that God closes, there are other doors that He will knock down or push open for us. For every door He leaves open, He will have the right people in place to be a blessing. God's plan helps us avoid the enemy's traps and reset the right priorities.

Life Point # 16

God can open and close doors at will. Stop giving the devil credit for every door that is shut. Some of those doors God closes and opens for a reason. Be willing to accept God's truth and move according to His excellent timing.

"Commit to the Lord whatever you do, and your plans will succeed" (*Prov. 16:3*) (**NLT**).

The best way to have success is for God to order our steps. When God orders your steps, your plans line up with His plans. When God guides you, your plan will line up with His purpose and His will. We realize that our plans are not about what we want to see happen for us as much as it is about what God will make happen for us. My plans are no longer created by the *D. Cassagnol Show*. Instead, my plans are sponsored by what God has already spoken. My plans must be about God's will for me. It is His show.

"In their hearts humans plan their course, but God establishes their steps" (*Prov. 16:9*) (NIV).

You can make all the plans that you want, but it is the Lord who makes everything happen. That is why your success is *not* based on your plans. Your success is based on what God wants to put in motion for you. You may have a plan in your heart, but it is God who establishes the course of action. He is the God of resources, and everything belongs to Him. God is the architect and builder of our lives.

"The earth is the Lord's, and the fullness thereof, the world and all who dwell therein" (*Ps. 24:1*).

Reflection Point 8—God will never fail.

No matter what the circumstances, we must keep our faith and trust in God. Failing is not an option with God. He is a firm foundation. If your hope is built on anything else besides God, then you are walking on sinking sand. Remember God will not fail because God cannot fail. Man may fail in his efforts to get things done but not God. Even when man fails, God knows how to take those failures and disappointments and make everything work out for the good. God told Joshua that "I would never fail thee; I will not forsake thee" (Josh. 1:5).

Take a few moments and reflect on God's faithfulness. There were situations that you could not have made it through without God's help or favor. People in your life had already turned their thumbs down on you, but God flipped the script. Those promotions, bonuses, accolades, and achievements were not possible without God's unmerited benevolence. Where would we be if not for the Lord's grace and mercy?

I would have never been able to author this book without God's approval and His numerous contributions. I thank God for the many people that He placed in my path. I am grateful for their kindness, support, and love. I thank God for the tears shed along the way. God knew that I needed spiritual toughening. Despite my brokenness, emptiness, and despair, God never left me. God lifted my discouragement and propelled me forward in all my seasons. My smiles today are because of His promises. God never fails.

"Not one word of all the good promises that the Lord had made to the house of Israel had failed; all came to pass" (*Josh. 21:45*).

"But as for you, ye thought evil against me, but God meant it unto good, to bring to pass, as it is this day, to save much people alive" (*Gen. 50:20*).

David knew that God was with him. David was not a physical match to Goliath. The armor that Saul offered him did not fit. The soldiers, including his brothers, thought that David did not stand a chance against the battle-hardened Goliath. In fact, Goliath was insulted that the Israelites would even send a puny boy to fight him. But David knew that his size did not matter. He knew that his success was not about the rock that he used to kill Goliath. David knew that God was with him. He knew that God would protect him. Later in David's life, he admitted that he had never seen the righteous forsaken or his seed begging bread (Ps. 37:25). David knew that he could trust God because He never fails.

Reflection Point 9 God will fight for us.

Imagine someone foolish enough to challenge the wrecking power of God. It sounds absurd, but the Bible has plenty of examples of people and nations that did. When you trust God and are obedient to His purpose and plans, then God will cover you. Even if His plans lead you into battle, you do not have to worry. God will march into that battle and fight boldly for you. It does not matter who tries to attack or castigate you, they will be defeated.

God told Joshua that no one would stand up against him (Josh. 1:5). Joshua knew that it was not his strength or ability that would procure victory for the Israelites. Joshua relied totally on God. As long as they were obedient, Joshua knew that God would be with him during every battle and cause them to win each war. All the kings and people of the land of Canaan were defeated because God fought for Israel (Josh. 10:42).

God will fight for you if you are willing to wait on Him. Do not rush God to exterminate everybody that you feel has done you wrong. Instead, be willing to wait on God's timing as He executes His plans for you. You don't have to be afraid of how things look. God is not intimidated by people or the size of your problem. God will defend and work things out for you.

"Do not be afraid of them; the Lord your God himself will fight for you" (*Deut. 3:22*) **(NIV).**

"For the Lord your God is the one who goes with you to fight for you against your enemies to give you victory" (*Deut. 20:4*) **(NIV).**

Don't try to control or aggravate the situation. God does not want you to interfere with what He is trying to do. Your job is to trust the Lord with unwavering doubt in His ability to help you conquer your circumstances. Confess and repent of any sin in your life. Remember God will fight for you, but disobedience will not be tolerated. The Israelites should have been able to demolish Ai the first time. However, due to Achan's sin (Josh. 7:19-20), they were defeated.

Meditating on an infallible and immutable God makes it easier for us to wait. These reflection points remind us that God is with us in the wait. Knowing that God is clearing the way and that there is no one greater than Him fortifies and invigorates. God is our refuge and a strong tower that we can run into and be safe (Prov.18:10).

Chapter 5

Empowered in the Wait

There is a myriad of benefits for waiting on God. We need to know that we cannot beat God's ability to bless us. When we wait on God, we win. We gain clarity and reassurance in our situation. We find out who we are and what we are made of. We evaluate our character and serve as bold witnesses. Our discernment and strength come from our time spent with God. As God manifests the blessing, our trust is built. If God does not produce the things that we have asked for, we still can have hope in knowing that He has something better. We gain strength because we know that God hears us and, in His timing, will answer. We are no longer fearful because we know that God is our defense. We may feel weak initially, but we know that our help comes from the Lord. Just communing with Him brings peace, comfort, and joy.

There are many biblical characters who waited on God despite unsurmountable odds. These people were faithful to fulfill God's objective. They were strengthened and rewarded for their diligence. These are just a few:

Joseph

God propelled Joseph from the pit to the palace. Joseph was willing to wait on God to manifest his dreams. No matter how silly they may have sounded to his father and brothers, Joseph knew that his future dreams would become a reality. His father and brothers did not realize that one day Joseph would be in a position of power. He would be able to rescue them from famine. Joseph never gave up or allowed anyone to discourage him. He waited on God to elevate him (Gen. chapters 37—39).

David

Samuel had anointed David as King Saul's successor. David was anointed king while he was still a shepherd living at his father's house. He could have gotten the big head after he was anointed as the next king or after he fought Goliath. But he did not. David went back to the fields and hillsides and assumed his role as a shepherd. David understood that God had more in store for him, but he would have to wait. He could have disparaged Jonathan since he knew that King Saul's son would not inherit the kingdom from his father. David did not. Knowing that he was going to be the next king, David could have killed Saul inside the cave. He knew the importance of waiting on God. He waited for God to place him as king. (1 Sam. 16:1–13; 24:10; 2 Sam. 5:1–5). Even after David became king, he still realized the importance of waiting on God to help him make the right decisions. David inquired of the Lord what he should do. He asked God whether he should fight the Philistines and then waited for an answer. He asked Him whether he should pursue after the Amalekites and then waited for an answer. God is not afraid to battle and does not need our help to win. God will fight to fulfill His purpose.

Eliezer

Eliezer waited for God to help him find a wife for his master Abraham's son. Eliezer was the chief or senior servant. He had worked for Abraham for a long time. He knew that Abraham did not want him to select a foreign woman. Abraham required him to search for a wife who was not a Canaanite. The woman had to be from Abraham's family. Eliezer waited on God to help him find Rebecca for Isaac (Gen. 24:12–27).

The Israelites

The walls of Jericho came down as the children of Israel followed God's plan. They waited on the Lord's plan to destroy the walls. They were obedient. God brought those walls down after seven days. The Israelites were instructed to march around the city walls quietly for the first six days. On the seventh day, the Lord told them to shout. Had the children of Israel decided to shout on the fourth day, God would not have manifested the promise. Had the children of Israel marched around only two days and taken a break, then God would not have worked on their behalf. They knew that they needed to be obedient to God's instruction and wait on God's timing to bring down those fortified walls (Josh. 6:1–27).

Each of these characters could have easily executed a different plan and taken an easier route. But they would have not received the Lord's blessing if they had not waited on God. They were faithful to fulfill God's objective in their life. Both David and Joseph had key leadership roles. They realized the significance of staying on track and not allowing the enemy to persuade them otherwise.

The story would have been different had Joseph succumbed to the flesh with Potiphar's wife. What would have happened had David killed Saul when he had the chance or tried to usurp King Saul's authority before God's timing? What would have happened if Eliezer gave up his search and returned empty-handed despite the promise that he made? The Israelites knew that the only way those impenetrable walls were going to come down was to do it God's way. God said march around, and they marched. God said be quiet until the seventh day and then shout. That is what they did. They held onto God's promise and did not doubt God.

We can learn from the experiences of these characters. The lessons we can learn are:

- ❖ No matter what the situation looks like, God will always be there for us.

- ❖ Always trust God and give God the glory.

- ❖ God's timing is always the best timing.

- ❖ When you wait on God, you do not have to settle for anything.

- ❖ Waiting on God helps you turn your attention to the future.

- ❖ Waiting on God gets you the best results.

- ❖ God knows how to tear down walls that are obstacles for you.

Chapter 6

Failure to Wait (The Downside of the Wait)

When we do not wait on God, we often hinder God's plans for us. Although no one can stop God's plans, we create mistakes or problems that hurt us and impact others. We cannot out-bless God. God's ways are always the best option. When we do not wait on God, we miss it; we do not choose God's best for us. We prolong our blessings and must retake the test. We end up experiencing more adversity and we extend our time in disappointment. We play into the enemy's trap, and we do not win.

God's plan must reign in our lives. But if God's plan does not rule, then someone else's plan does. When we fail to wait on God to manifest His plan or to rule, we institute our own ideas. When we are governed by our selfish desires, disaster usually prevails.

The downside of the wait is believing that the only way things will happen is if we make them happen. The downside of the wait is assuming that God is unable to keep His promises and that God does not understand or want you to experience positive outcomes. As a result, you feel obligated to take charge and move ahead of God. You think that your solution will fulfill your desires and bring you a great reward. We eventually discover, the hard way, that all things do *not* work together for good when we advance our shortsighted plans.

The wait is supposed to teach us to trust God. The wait grooms us for the next level and shows us how to enlarge our faith. The wait should not be considered as a negative aspect of receiving from the Lord. Instead, the wait is God's expected time needed for our beneficial growth as we trust God's mighty and timely alternatives for us.

These are just a few of the biblical characters who did not wait on God:

Sarah

Life Point # 17

If you are feeling stressed, hopeless, and lack peace, recommend the presence of the Lord! Spending time with God correctly colors the situation. Waiting in the safety of the Lord helps you find the proper perspective.

God promised Sarah that she would have a child. Sarah did not initially receive what God was saying. In fact, she laughed. Sarah thought conception at her age (ninety) was an impossibility. Sarah felt that the only way for her to have a child was through surrogacy. Sarah did not wait on God to manifest the promise. She devised a plan to have a child by her servant. There were several problems generated by her plan. Sarah was jealous and mistreated Hagar. Hagar was slighted and eventually despised Sarah and ran away. Ishmael did not gain Sarah's favor and became collateral damage. Ishmael and Israel did not get along as boys and were even enemies in future generations. Abraham, tired of the whole situation, punted the responsibility concerning Hagar back to Sarah. What a mess! Sarah's plan caused pain for herself, Hagar, Ishmael, Isaac, and Abraham (Gen. 16:1–16).

Absalom

Absalom is a perfect example of what happens when we are rebellious and do not consult or wait on God to help us deal with our

Failure to Wait (The Downside of the Wait)

issues. Ammon, Absalom's half-brother, raped Tamar. Tamar was Absalom's sister. Absalom felt that Ammon should marry her rather than allow her to live a life of disgrace. Absalom told his father what Ammon had done. He hoped that David would punish Ammon. When David refused to act, Absalom took matters into his own hands. Absalom was angry and decided to retaliate. Instead of taking the issue to God and waiting on God's vindication, Absalom murdered Ammon. Additionally, Absalom wanted to be David's replacement. He never consulted his father about who David wanted to be the next king of Israel. Absalom never consulted God about his desire to be the next king. Absalom dishonored his father by sleeping with his concubines. Absalom disparaged his father to the people and plotted to kill David. Absalom tried to win the people's hearts so that he would be the next king. Absalom failed to wait on God's guidance. Absalom's plan backfired. He never became king and was killed instead. (2 Sam. chapters 13–19)

Life Point # 18

Do not tie a brick to a sling shot expecting great progress. The rock is not going far and you might end up hurting yourself and others. Wait for God's approval and let Him elevate you. Stop trying to promote your agenda. God can put you in position and successfully keep you there according to His timing.

King Saul

Sometimes God is trying to teach us patience or evaluate our character during the wait. Saul was impatient and found it difficult to wait for the prophet Samuel to join him at Gilgal. Instead of waiting on Samuel to conduct the sacrifice, Saul decided to conduct the ceremony. The Lord did not want Saul to offer the sacrifice. Samuel told him to wait seven days until he arrived. Although Saul waited seven days, he failed to wait for the

> *Life Point # 19*
>
> *We open ourselves to unnecessary attacks and devastating consequences when we lack self-control in executing our plans. There is always a shattering aftermath when we enforce our way over God's way. (Proverbs 25:8)*

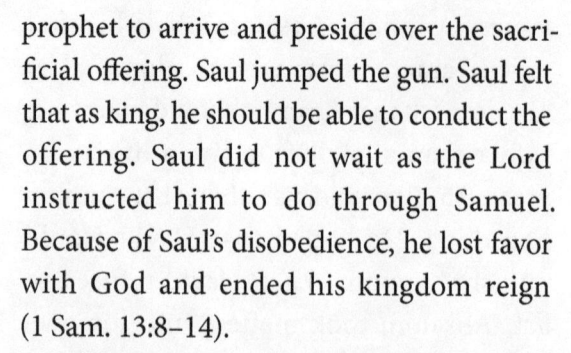

prophet to arrive and preside over the sacrificial offering. Saul jumped the gun. Saul felt that as king, he should be able to conduct the offering. Saul did not wait as the Lord instructed him to do through Samuel. Because of Saul's disobedience, he lost favor with God and ended his kingdom reign (1 Sam. 13:8–14).

These characters paid a heavy price for their disobedience and failure to wait on God. They hurt others, fell out of favor, and lost position. In each case, they felt that they could solve their own problems and took matters into their own hands. Instead of waiting on God's plan, they did what they thought was best.

Lessons that we learned are:

- ❖ Obedience is better than sacrifice.

- ❖ Be of good courage and wait on the Lord.

- ❖ We mess up when we take matters into our own hands.

Failure to Wait (The Downside of the Wait)

- ❖ Do not put God in a box.

- ❖ Do not expect God to operate, based on your timing.

- ❖ Even when you cannot see God moving, you still need to believe that He is looking out for you.

- ❖ Your actions can create problems and wreak havoc in your life and others.

- ❖ God is mindful of you and will provide all that you need.

- ❖ Trust God to give you the desires of your heart.

- ❖ Do not let others pressure you into doing things that will get you in trouble with God.

Chapter 7

Confirm your Wait (Questions That Position You for the Wait)

How many times have you said, "If I would have just waited on God, then things would be different," or "I would not be in this mess if I would have just turned to God for help." Some of us are still kicking ourselves when we think about how things could have been so much better had we waited on God to guide the situation. Perhaps, you recall how much money and time you could have saved if you would have just waited on God. Some personal relationships would still be flourishing or would have ended much sooner had we either consulted or waited on God. Regrets! Regrets and Regrets!

Go ahead and be honest. If you missed an opportunity to wait on God and you did your own thing, just own it. Contrary to what you thought might happen, you learned the hard way that God already knew what was going to happen. Unfortunately, you did not realize your reality until it smacked you in the face. Consider this, God does not charge a consultation fee. We can talk to God at any time for free. Now that you have learned and know better, you will not get stuck in situational quicksand.

Here are some questions that you can ask yourself prior to making those decisions so that you will not be tempted to move ahead of God:

- Do you know the future?

- Are you perfect and without fault?

- Are you 100 percent sure that the person or people you trust will never hurt or disappoint you?

- Are you 100 percent certain that your solution is a "God" solution?

- Are you 100 percent sure that the decision or move that you are about to make is something that God would recommend for you at this time?

- Will you be able to quickly recover physically, mentally, emotionally, financially, and spiritually?

- Can you make people do or think what you want them to do or think in this situation?

Confirm your Wait (Questions That Position You for the Wait)

- Will this decision prompt a fight that you are not ready to have?

- Are you trying to self-destruct, and do you want to intentionally shipwreck?

- Can you manage every circumstance that develops with the implementation of your plan?

If you answered "no" to any of the above questions, then that is enough proof to validate the fact that you need to consult the Lord and wait on Him. You need a God answer. You are tired of losing or experiencing sporadic wins. It is time to redistribute the odds. With God, you can win all the time. Take a few moments to reflect on those questions. Feel free to use the spaces to briefly describe the time you did not wait on God. If the questions are applicable, use the spaces to write about your experiences.

Since you do not have God's omniscience or his access to the future, slow your roll and wait on Him. There is no way that you can predict the future, and you certainly are not perfect. There is no way that you can guarantee that people you trust will not hurt you. Even if you can make an acceptable and practical guess, it will be a partial one at best. Unlike God, you are not privy to all the outside factors. God heard the late-night conversations and the pillow talk. He knows how people honestly feel about you. He knows the real deal.

When you act without God, you need to stop and consider that there are too many possibilities that might cause you to miss something in your misguided calculation. There are too many things that you do not know about. Besides when relying on others, you have no clue about the intents of someone's heart. You cannot figure everybody out. You are working with limited knowledge. In many cases, you are acting based on emotions, disguised admiration, doubletalk, and personal perception. In the wait, you can find out who the people are whom God has placed in your path to bless you. In the wait, you can discover God's plan and strategy for you.

Are people really helping you because they genuinely want to see you do better? Maybe they are open and receptive to you because of what you bring to the table. After you are no longer useful to them, they discard you like yesterday's trash. Many have been deceived by fruitless words and false pretenses. But God is never fooled. God knows where you stand with others. God can help you discern if that relationship is a fruitful investment or not.

You do not have the power over others to make them think the way you want them to. You are not able to control minds like a Jedi in *Star Wars*. I have raised four children and now as adults, they do not always agree with my way of thinking. Who knew that they would grow up to have their own different opinions? Who knew that they would want to make their own choices and forget to call me before making major decisions? Who knew that their behavior would either make me proud or send me to my knees? In all accounts, God did. That is all the confirmation I need to wait on the Lord and trust His timely intervention in not only my life but the lives of my children as well.

All my husband and I could do was to pour into our children and deposit our best when they were little (Prov. 22:6). Now, we pray for them and try to make ourselves available to assist when we can. God knows we have no power over our adult children and others to make them act or think the way that we do. We can try to influence or persuade, but the choice is theirs to do as they see fit. God will have to do the rest.

Trusting and waiting on God can alleviate the need for control in a power struggle. Trusting in God shifts the interdependence on man

Confirm your Wait (Questions That Position You for the Wait)

to reliance on God. Waiting for God's answers solidifies your standing and helps you make the right choice.

We must wait on the Lord for guidance before the shipwreck. We do not have to wait for all hell to break loose before we call on the Lord. We must talk to God and apply God's Word. Good solutions can help, but God's solutions are always better. God's solutions are complete, permanent, and will take you so much further.

Other questions that you might want to consider during the wait as you are learning about God's will for you are:

Will others be affected by your decision?

My husband says, "What you do always affects someone else." There is a great deal of truth wrapped up in that statement. When we make mistakes, there is always somebody else who feels the agony and inadvertently experiences the struggle with you. When you share confidences and that information is used indiscreetly, you are not the only one who is affected. When you choose to accept employment that does not cover your expenses or work extremely long hours, experience health issues, join the wrong organization, commit a crime, marry the wrong person, suffer from addictions, spend money foolishly, provoke arguments, separate, or get a divorce, and so on, there are others who will be caught up in the conflict as well.

Do you want to make a long-lasting, positive difference in the lives of others?

Sure, you do. That is why we need God to help us, so we will not mess up our lives and the lives of others. We are role models. There are people looking up to us and will use our lives as examples. As role models, we want to participate and volunteer to support community activities like the local foodbanks, youth sport's leagues, pet shelters, habitat for humanity, homeless missions, city zoo, botanical gardens, as well as visit veteran facilities, nursing homes, and hospitals, read to young people at the library, join and serve at the United Service Organization and in the various ministries at your church, and build a life legacy that others will cherish and emulate.

As a leader, you should train others. You can spend quality time through mentorship at the church or boys' and girls' club. Here is where you really get a chance to mold and teach life experiences. Here is where you can help people develop and grow as you acknowledge shortcomings and strengths that have either hurt or helped you to become successful. Ask God to help you share some of your past mistakes with others. Believe it or not, your mistakes can be someone else's lifeline. God will let you know the audience that can be helped and encouraged by your testimony. Sometimes, it is not expedient for you to share everything with everyone. People tend to harbor grudges, fixate on retaliation, and use the information to hurt you. So always ask God when, where, and with whom should you share.

"He that walketh with wise men shall be wise: but a companion of fools shall be destroyed" (*Prov. 13:20*).

"In all things show yourself to be an example of good deeds, with purity in doctrine, dignified, sound in speech which is beyond reproach, so that the opponent will be put to shame, having nothing bad to say about us" (*Titus 2:7-8*).

Obviously, there are no perfect parents. Hopefully, we will take the time to talk to our own children about our lives to include some of the mistakes. This will show our loved ones that we are human and that we also need God's help. Apologize for hurtful mistakes and maltreatment of others. Hopefully, our children will see that we are human and that we, too, must trust God for a better solution.

"Train up a child in the way he should go: and when he is old, he will not depart from it" (*Prov. 22:6*).

"And ye shall teach them your children, speaking of them when thou sittest in thine house, and when thou walkest by the way, when thou liest down, and when thou risest up" (*Deut. 11:19*).

Do you want to contribute to generational blessings?

We need to leave a godly legacy and a heritage for our children. Many generational blessings were the direct result of the prayers and godly lifestyles of past family members carving out a lasting heritage. Unfortunately, the same can be said about generational curses. We must start now, teaching our children godly principles. Joshua said, "As for me and my house we are going to serve the Lord." The enemy does not stop trying to destroy only you; he targets your seed as well. We must live godly examples by exemplifying Christ and thinking about the best way to help our children. We are the salt of the earth and the light of the world (Matt. 5:13–16).

Are you in right fellowship/relationship with God?

If you have not confessed any sin, then you must do so. You need your prayers to get through to God. You do not want anything to serve as an impediment to getting God's answer. You want to be grounded and maintain a healthy relationship with the Lord on a regular basis and not just when you need something. Are you reading and following His Word? God wants you to be more than just a hearer of the Word. He wants you to be a doer (James 1: 22–25).

Have you prayed, searched the Word, or shared with a God appointed vessel?

God's word has the answer. God has seasoned people that you can turn to for advice. You can ask them to pray with you and for you. Their advice must line up with God's Word. Ask God to send you someone who knows His Word and has the maturity level and compassion to deal with your problem. If they do not have the maturity level, then they will mishandle the confidential information. If they do not have compassion, then their truth will be delivered in a hurtful way. They will abuse and betray your confidence. You will have a tough time trusting others. If you are not sure about who to talk to, you can talk to a very close friend, your pastor, or designated representative. Additionally, your parents and spouse should be people in which you can confide.

Are you willing to surrender and let God have his way?

Make sure your will aligns with God's will. You do not have time to ask amiss or reject God's will. Life is short, so you do not have time to make wrong choices. Wrong choices can reroute your course and take you from your goal.

Even if you answered "Yes, No, or I do not know" to the above considerations, you still need to wait on God. Remember there are no exemptions. When we wait on God, we experience the best outcome for our situation. God produces sustainable results. He is a difference maker. Many times, we rely on hindsight. We try to learn from our mistakes after the fact. God's vision is spot on. God has the hindsight and foresight. His peripheral vision is 100 percent accurate, and He can see all around your situation. In the wait, you can verify what God wants you to do. God can answer your questions. You do not have to guess or take any chances. God wants you to recognize His voice and have His assurance. That is why we must wait on Him.

Chapter 8

Make The Wait Count

The ideal situation would be to pray one night and have the answer to that prayer come the next morning. Wouldn't it be something if that happened? But that rarely happens. In many cases, there is a longer waiting period between the time that you send the prayer out and the time that God answers. Now, the time in between the prayer and the answer is the "wait time." Unfortunately, it is this time that many of us waste.

Instead of viewing this time as a negative or dormant part of your life, you should think of the wait time as a time to invest or get involved in the things that please the Lord. If you are already involved, then do not quit. Constant crying while pleading your case is mentally and emotionally draining. Yelling, threatening, and getting angry with God is also a waste of time. You may have vented, but the problem is still there. Pouting, turning your back to the wall, getting people to feel sorry for you, and refusing to eat like King Ahab (1 Kings 21:4–5) is not the way to act.

Instructing God on the best way to fix your situation does not work and will not make God move any faster. God does not want us to lose hope as we wait on Him. The average human gestational period is nine months. The average wait time for a baccalaureate degree is four years. There are twelve grades in addition to nursery and preschool. There are twelve months of wait time for all sports at the collegiate and national level before a champion is crowned. There are four years of competitive training between each of the Olympic games.

These are a few examples of wait times. Yes, a lot happens during the wait. However, at the end of the waiting period, the desired results make for a momentous occasion. We cannot afford to give up during the wait. Knowing that God is with us during the wait is a powerful source of comfort and reassurance.

Hope deferred makes the heart sick, but a longing fulfilled is a tree of life (Prov.13:12). (NIV)

"Be joyful in hope, patient in affliction, faithful in prayer" (Rom. 12:12).

While you are waiting on God, you must encourage yourself in the Lord. Do not wait for someone else to throw you a lifeline. When the people were ready to stone David for their loss, David had to encourage himself in the Lord (1 Sam. 30:6). David did not rely or wait on anyone else to get him through his grief.

You can achieve the win out of your situation and make the wait count by following these goals:

Waiting Goal 1 Live by Faith

Believe God is going to answer your prayer. Be proactive. Take your stand at the watch post and begin looking for signs of what God is doing. You already know that God is the only one who can answer prayers. He is in the healing and deliverance business. God said in His Word (Phil. 1:6) that He will finish the work that He started in you. While you are waiting, enter this period with the expectation that God is going to complete His work in you. Whatever is needed to make that happen, God is going to see to it that it happens. As you are trusting God, He is finalizing His plans.

As you wait patiently and confidently, you can expect God's goodness in your situation. Despite what you see or how you feel, believe that God hears you and is working on your behalf. When you demonstrate your faith in God, you encourage others. Paul and Silas singing songs of praise in the prison served to encourage the other prisoners (Acts

16:23–33). The inmates were amazed at how they could rejoice after being beaten and placed in stocks. I believe that even before God sent the earthquake at midnight, the actions of Paul and Silas could have caused the other inmates to later make up their minds to give their lives to the Lord. Your faith serves as a living testament toward the goodness of God. You have no idea of all the people who might be impacted by your life. God wants people who trust Him and are willing to exemplify their faith as they wait on Him to answer their prayers. God wants people that trust Him and are willing to draw closer to Him.

Waiting Goal 2 Pray, Be Thankful, and Read the Word of God

Never stop praying. Praying and begging are different. Praying purges and purifies while begging is repressive and produces anxiety. After you have given your request to the Lord, then keep praying for others. Pray for your family members, church, job, school, and leaders in government. There are so many situations that you can pray for besides just your request.

Start thanking and praising God in advance. God's credit is phenomenal, and His satisfaction rate is unparalleled. It is God's will for you to be thankful in all circumstances. Murmuring and complaining will not get you anywhere. We need to think positive. Positive thoughts encourage you and build your endurance. Positive thoughts help to keep your focus and trust on God instead of your circumstances. Do not worry about how God is going to do it; just thank God for seeing you through it.

The Bible says think on the things that are "true, noble, right, pure, lovely, admirable, and praiseworthy" (Phil. 4:8). When we think differently, we start doubting God. When we start doubting God, we move from a place of waiting to manipulating. We move from God's plan to our plan. How can you pray in the Spirit on all occasions for all the Lord's people when you have decided to abandon God's plan and do your own thing? How are you encouraging others to wait on the Lord when you are not waiting?

Some situations may require fasting to go along with your prayer. As you are praying, do not make a public display. Pray secretly and God will reward openly. When you pray, tell God how precious His thoughts are concerning you. Let God know that you realize that all of God's thoughts are good towards you and that even in the darkened situation, you know that God is there.

Pray that God will open your understanding as you read His Word. We must read the Word of God. The Word of God is active, alive, and judges the thoughts and the attitudes of the heart. The Word of God provides clear direction. God speaks through His Word. The Bible provides wisdom, encouraging scriptures, admonishments, and situational and personal outcomes.

Waiting Goal 3 Keep Serving God

Do not quit on God. Be faithful to honor your commitments. While you are waiting on God to fulfil the promise, do not stop going to church. If you are serving, continue to serve. Do not stop singing in the choir or playing in the church band. The enemy would love nothing more than for you to walk away from God. The devil wants you to lose your mind and act foolishly. The enemy will tell you to go rogue since God did not answer your prayer. But this is the time where you continue to work and fellowship with others. Be an example. Continue to preach and teach God's Word. Continue to exemplify Christ. Continue to pray for the people of God. Continue to operate the food bank and visit the sick. God sees what you are doing. Remember the reaping and sowing principle. Get involved with various outreach programs. You will discover that it is a blessing to serve and give to others.

Understand that there are not many people who enjoy waiting. It is uncomfortable and causes anxiety. However, you need to be willing to wait on God to manifest the promise or the requested prayer. While you are waiting, that is not the time to turn your back on God. That is not the time to start doubting God. Maintain your commitments and keep serving. You will be abundantly blessed.

"Therefore, my beloved brethren, be ye steadfast, unmovable, always abounding in the work of the Lord, for as much as ye know that your labor is not in vain in the Lord" (*1ˢᵗ Cor. 15:58*).

Waiting Goal 4 Remember What God Has Already Done

Talk about the goodness of God. Reflect on the trials and the tests that God has already seen you through. You will not be able to count all your blessings. I remember the time that I received a report that my oldest daughter was going to be deformed. I cried for three nights over that diagnosis. Thankfully, my husband never received that report. He would always say, "Whose report are we going to believe? I choose to believe the report of the Lord." His strong conviction and dedication of faith as well as the prayers of our pastor, his wife, and congregation tremendously blessed me through that test.

I began speaking life and praying wholeness over my womb. I remember praying for strength to deal with the situation. I prayed for wisdom to accept God's will for my situation. Prayer works. When the baby was born, she weighed 6 pounds and 12 ounces. . She was twenty-two inches long. Joy was a pretty baby girl with a head full of hair. The medical report initially said that the baby would be deformed. The doctor claimed that they had administered the alpha feta protein test too early. He said that was the reason for the faulty reading. I did not argue with the doctor. I was too busy praising and thanking God for the victory report.

That incident happened thirty-two years ago, but I still remember it. That testimony and countless others continue to bless me and many others. Like the children of Israel, I pulled out my stone and used it as a memorial and testament to the goodness of God. God has been faithful through the generations. He blesses you and your family.

Remember the shared testimonies of victory and not defeat. Denounce what the enemy is trying to do. Through prayer and speaking God's Word, tear down the strongholds that exalts itself against the knowledge of God. Use the power of your testimony to uplift God and refute the enemy.

Waiting Goal 5 Quote Encouraging Scriptures and Affirmations

Remind yourself what the Word says about what God can do for the believers. The Word says that you are not weak because God strengthens you. The Word reinforces the fact that the favor of the Lord is upon you. It proves to you that God wants you to prosper and be successful. The Lord is your shepherd and you will not lack or be in need. God will look out for you, and there is no need for you to be afraid. The Lord hears your cry and comes to see you. God orders your steps. You can commit to God, and He will establish your plans. The more you speak God's Word, the more confidence you will have to stand up like a mounted eagle. You will not be weary or faint.

The more you read the Word, the more enhanced your prayer life will be. Speaking the Word in your prayers strengthens your faith, neutralizes, and redirects self-exaltation. Suddenly, you begin to realize that the struggle that you have is not about your ability to control the situation. Instead, it is about putting your focus on God's ability and letting Him maneuver the struggle. Speaking the Word highlights and affirms God. God's role is increased while your role is decreased. Quoting scriptures when you pray not only encourages you but reminds God that you are aware of His promises. God will not be offended if you repeat His Word back to him.

As you read, study, and memorize the scriptures, do not forget to apply them daily. Turn the scriptures into declarations that you can use to uplift and encourage yourself and others. Recently, my youngest daughter wrote and submitted these tips and affirmations to be included in a brochure in a women's conference.

Encourage Godly Waiting

Write them on your mirror, repeat them aloud on the way to work, or recite them with your family. However, you choose to speak to that mountain, speak to it with intention and expectancy. Know that anything that you think, you can see. Anything you want, you can acquire. Anything you pursue, you can perfect. The brain believes exactly what you tell it, so tell it this:

1. I love to wait on God!

2. I have everything I need.

3. I'm right where God wants me.

4. I expect to experience God's blessings every day!

5. I know the victory is already mine!

6. I rejoice at all times because God is constantly showing up for me!

7. I value and place priority on spending time with God daily.

8. Consulting with God fulfils me in a supernatural way.

9. I rest peacefully because I allow God to fight my battles.

10. Everything is working in my favor.

God Bless you!
Sister Glory

When I visited her, I was inspired by the number of amazing pronouncements that Glory had written on sticky notes and placed them around her house. She said she was fueled to write these positive expressions while reading the book of Psalms. She admitted that these statements helped her through some challenging times. You can do the same. Just read the Word or inspirational passages from other books and begin to meditate on the goodness of God. Write down what the Word is saying. You will be surprised at how many affirmations you will create. Post them in various places where you can read them. Reflect on them and repeat them aloud.

Waiting Goal 6 Sing and Dance to Praise Songs

Life Point # 20

You can be strengthened and encouraged in the Lord by singing songs that minister healing and wholeness. Listen to the uplifting words exalting God in the song. Those celebratory lyrics boast on the promises of God.

Singing and dancing to praise songs helps you to maintain your focus on God. They help you to exhalt and esteem the Lord. It is difficult to ask God to help you get over past relationships while you are singing the same old worldly songs that you used to sing when you were in that relationship. Let us face it; love songs are not written to put you in the mood to praise the Lord. Worldly songs are not going to tell you that God is a rock or a source of strength in moments of weakness. Carnal songs are going to tell you to do your own thing. Some carnal songs help you to shake your groove thing and serve to remind you of a self-driven and ruthless past. In many cases, carnal songs promote lust, greed, and covetousness wrapped up in lyrics with mesmerizing vocals and award-winning music. I like watching smooth dance moves and listening to cool rhythmic beats. However, I have found that not all songs promote an environment that is conducive to worship. Worldly songs are not designed to help you get your praise on or think about the Lord.

Waiting Goal 7 Spend Time with People Who Genuinely Support You

God did not plan for us to spend life alone. We need life partners or groups to connect with. These groups will pray and encourage you to apply God's Word in your life. Find people with a kindred spirit to share what God is doing in your life. Be careful about sharing your aspirations and dreams with everyone. Not everyone is happy or wishes the best for you. Find someone who is praying for you and not preying on you. Find someone who is genuinely supportive and not superficial. Birds of a feather flock together for a reason.

When you are struggling, there will be someone there to pray for you and offer a word of encouragement. When you fall, these people will help pick you up. They will not condemn or be judgmental. Instead, they will be reminded of their own testimony and know what God did for them. They will be empathetic and show compassion. But for God's grace, we would face a life of doom. People that do not understand or believe in the power of God will not promote God's way over what they think is best.

As we wait for God to change our situations, we must learn how to make the wait count. Practicing these waiting goals will help you to grow as you wait and show you how to wait right.

Chapter 9

Wait In The Word

We must trust God during the waiting seasons of our life. God is showing us how to depend on Him and become more like Christ. There are plenty of examples of biblical characters who waited on God to receive the promised blessings. Unfortunately, the people who did not wait on God suffered the consequences. Always remember that God never fails. He is going to do what He says He will do. We must be steadfast and wait on Him.

Think about the people in your life, who have waited on God. What was their testimony like versus people who did not wait on God?

This chapter includes twenty scriptures that will encourage you to wait on the Lord. These scriptures will help you endure the wait as you trust God for the answer. These scriptures will remind you to be strengthened and encouraged as you experience life's challenges. Recite and pray these scriptures as you wait on God. Keep them in your heart as you go through your tests.

To be *in the wait* means that you are in position to experience God's presence and power. As you meditate and read the word of God, God is renewing and recharging that space in your heart that yearns to please Him. To be *in the wait* means that you are waiting in the word which closes you off from worldly concerns and safeguards you from the enemy's deceptive tactics and distraction. Being **in the wait** spiritually brings you into an area of protection where inner peace and freedom from fear and hurt dwell. When you are *in the wait*, you are surrounded by God's love and understanding which invites openness and furthers relationship.

All these scriptures are from the New International Version (NIV) Bible or the King James Version (KJV) Bible.

> Isaiah 40:31—But those who hope (wait) in the Lord will renew their strength. They will soar on wings like eagles; they will run and not grow weary; they will walk and not faint.
>
> Psalm 31:24—Be strong and take heart, all you who hope (wait) in the Lord.
>
> Psalm 33:20—We wait in hope for the Lord; he is our help and our shield.
>
> Psalm 52: 9—For what you have done I will always praise you in the presence of your faithful people. And I will hope (wait) in your name, for your name is good.
>
> Psalm 130:5—I wait for the Lord, my whole being waits, and in his word, I put my hope.
>
> Psalm 40:1—I waited patiently for the Lord; he turned to me and heard my cry.
>
> Psalm 25:4–5—Show me your ways, Lord teach me your paths. Guide me in your truth and teach me, for you are God my Savior, and my hope is in you all day long.

Habakkuk 2:3—For the revelation (vision) awaits an appointed time; it speaks of the end and will not prove false. Though it linger, wait for it; it will certainly come and will not delay.

Proverbs 20:22—Do not say, "I'll pay you back for this wrong!" Wait for the Lord, and he will avenge you.

Psalm 38:15—Lord, I wait for you; you will answer, Lord my God.

Isaiah 8:17—I will wait for the Lord, who is hiding his face from the descendants of Jacob. I will put my trust in him.

1 Corinthians 1:7—Therefore you do not lack any spiritual gift as you eagerly wait for our Lord Jesus Christ to be revealed.

Romans 12:12—Be joyful in hope, patient in affliction, faithful in prayer.

Psalm 37:7—Be still before the Lord and wait patiently for him, do not fret when people succeed in their ways, when they carry out their wicked schemes.

Lamentations 3:25-26—The Lord is good to those who wait for him, to the soul; that seeking him. It is good that a man should both hope and quietly wait for the salvation of the Lord. (KJV)

James 1:12—Blessed is the one who perseveres under trial because, having stood the test, that person will receive the crown of life that the Lord has promised to those who love him.

Galatians 6:9—Let us not become weary in doing good, for at the proper time we will reap a harvest if we do not give up.

1 Peter 5:6—Humble yourselves, therefore, under God's mighty hand, that he may lift you up in due time.

Psalm 106:13—But they soon forgot what he had done and did not wait for his plan to unfold.

Micah 7:7—Therefore I will look unto the Lord: I will wait for the God of my salvation: my God will hear me (KJV).

Chapter 10

Let's Wait Together

Now that you know or have been reminded of the importance of the waiting process, you should be able to *wait* better. You also should be able to *wait* right. You know what to do while waiting, and you have begun memorizing, reciting, and speaking those wait scriptures (see chapter 9) so your whole stance on waiting should be different and improved. You have already started making your own reflections and posting them in your heart. You might have been impatient and doubtful before, but not anymore. Your waiting experience has helped you to connect with God in a way that has shifted and strengthened your overall faith position. Your waiting experience has catapulted to a whole other level. You have totally changed your perspective on waiting, and you are more inclined to waiting on the move of God with boldness and expectation.

In the wait you learned to spiritually dissect and examine your truth (sin nature) according to His word. As the Holy Spirit guided you in synchronizing His truth (righteousness) in your life, you were empowered and aligned your will with His. You have eliminated your excuses and are walking in agreement with God's purpose and plans. You wisely discerned (a fact that you've been resisting) that God's truth covers a larger view of the playing field and more than substantially exposes what is really going on in the physical and spiritual realm. **In**

the wait, you personally accepted the fact that God's truth, view, and choice always has the advantage and gives you the decisive edge.

The next time that you have a request or you are watching for God to fulfill a promise, you will wait with authority and commitment. You now have a new sense of clarity and yearning for God's awesome timing. We have been assured that God's timing is full of His wisdom and grace. God knows the best time for everything in every season. Nothing happens without his knowledge or his unlimited capacity to correct. We already know that He has the power to manifest His promises and bring them into existence for us. I used the pronoun *we* because waiting is a personal process that I must do as well.

Let us pray!

Most Gracious Heavenly Father,

We thank and praise you for what you have done and are planning to do in our lives. Because of you, we are excited about our future. We honor your awesome purpose and plans for us. Your plans come with peace, not evil and gives us an expected end. Help us not to be foolish or impatient as we wait on you. We know that when we wait on you by faith, we can call those things that are not as though they were. Lord, may we forever keep our hope and trust in you. May we forever wait *in* your word.

In Jesus name we pray,

Amen.

REFERENCES

"All scripture is from The King James Version (KJV) of the Bible., unless indicated otherwise. "New All scripture quotations are taken from the King James Version (KJV) of the Bible, New King James Version (NKJV), the New International Version (NIV), the New Living Translation (NLT) and the English Standard Version (ESV).

1. Tony Little, Ab Isolator Workout, Fitness Quest Inc. 1994, video, 50:32, https:youtube.com.

2. Civilla D. Martin, "His Eyes are on the Sparrow," arranged by Charles H. Gabriel, 1905, music video, 3:16, https:youtube.com/yFIH-K9JNWO.

3. Joyce Meyer, "God Wants to Do Life with Us!" September 17, 2022, video, 7:13, https://www.facebook.com/joycemeyerministries.

4. Andrea Moore (November 12, 2022) Summit Worship Center, Austin, Texas, https://www.summitatx.org.

5. Eric Moore (January 8, 2023) Summit Worship Center, Austin, Texas, https://www.summitatx.org.

6. Martha Munizzi , "Your Latter Will Be Greater, Best Is Yet to Come," Soundtrack, Say the Name Publishing/Martha Munizzi Music 2003, music video, 6:58, https:youtube.com/@marthamunizzi.

7. Mary Fishback Powers, "Footprints in the Sand," (Canada, HarperCollins Publishers Limited, January 1, 2002) p. 23.

8. Frank Sinatra, "My Way," Reprise Records, 1968, music video, 4:37, https://www. youtube.com.

9. Michael W. Smith, "Way Maker," Album Awaken: The Surrounded Experience, 2019, music video, 4:04, https://www.youtube.com

About the Author

Denise Cassagnol has been active in ministerial leadership for over thirty years. She is a retired teacher, former major in the US Army, motivational speaker, associate pastor, and co-founder of Kingdom Associates. Along with her husband, Pastor Antonio Cassagnol, she has been a dynamic leader and builder of High-Performance Teams. Together, they have worked diligently with pastors, leaders, and directors to promote and strategize productive and healthy organizations. She resides in El Paso, Texas, with her husband. They have four children, Marlon, Joy, Glory, and Tony. You can contact Denise at denisecassagnol@gmail.com.